MznLnx

Missing Links Exam Preps

Exam Prep for

Precalculus

Larson & Hostetler, 6th Edition

The MznLnx Exam Prep is your link from the texbook and lecture to your exams.
The MznLnx Exam Preps are unauthorized and comprehensive reviews of your textbooks.

All material provided by MznLnx and Rico Publications (c) 2010
Textbook publishers and textbook authors do not particpate in or contribute to these reviews.

MznLnx

Rico Publications

Exam Prep for Precalculus
6th Edition
Larson & Hostetler

Publisher: Raymond Houge
Assistant Editor: Michael Rouger
Text and Cover Designer: Lisa Buckner
Marketing Manager: Sara Swagger
Project Manager, Editorial Production: Jerry Emerson
Art Director: Vernon Lowerui

Product Manager: Dave Mason
Editorial Assitant: Rachel Guzmanji
Pedagogy: Debra Long
Cover Image: Jim Reed/Getty Images
Text and Cover Printer: City Printing, Inc.
Compositor: Media Mix, Inc.

(c) 2010 Rico Publications

ALL RIGHTS RESERVED. No part of this work covered by the copyright may be reproduced or used in any form or by an means--graphic, electronic, or mechanical, including photocopying, recording, taping, Web distribution, information storage, and retrieval systems, or in any other manner--without the written permission of the publisher.

Printed in the United States
ISBN:

For more information about our products, contact us at:
Dave.Mason@RicoPublications.com

For permission to use material from this text or product, submit a request online to:
Dave.Mason@RicoPublications.com

Contents

CHAPTER 1
Functions and Their Graphs — 1

CHAPTER 2
Polynomial and Rational Functions — 20

CHAPTER 3
Exponential and Logarithmic Functions — 36

CHAPTER 4
Trigonometry — 42

CHAPTER 5
Analytic Trigonometry — 55

CHAPTER 6
Additional Topics in Trigonometry — 59

CHAPTER 7
Systems of Equations and Inequalities — 70

ANSWER KEY — 90

TO THE STUDENT

COMPREHENSIVE

The *MznLnx* Exam Prep series is designed to help you pass your exams. Editors at MznLnx review your textbooks and then prepare these practice exams to help you master the textbook material. Unlike study guides, workbooks, and practice tests provided by the texbook publisher and textbook authors, *MznLnx* gives you **all** of the material in each chapter in exam form, not just samples, so you can be sure to nail your exam.

MECHANICAL

The MznLnx Exam Prep series creates exams that will help you learn the subject matter as well as test you on your understanding. Each question is designed to help you master the concept. Just working through the exams, you gain an understanding of the subject--its a simple mechanical process that produces success.

INTEGRATED STUDY GUIDE AND REVIEW

MznLnx is not just a set of exams designed to test you, its also a comprehensive review of the subject content. Each exam question is also a review of the concept, making sure that you will get the answer correct without having to go to other sources of material. You learn as you go! Its the easiest way to pass an exam.

HUMOR

Studying can be tedious and dry. MznLnx's instructional design includes moderate humor within the exam questions on occassion, to break the tedium and revitalize the brain

Chapter 1. Functions and Their Graphs

1. In mathematics and computer science, _____ (also base-16, hexa or base, of 16. It uses sixteen distinct symbols, most often the symbols 0-9 to represent values zero to nine, and A, B, C, D, E, F (or a through f) to represent values ten to fifteen.

   Its primary use is as a human friendly representation of binary coded values, so it is often used in digital electronics and computer engineering.

   a. Factoradic
   b. Tetradecimal
   c. Radix
   d. Hexadecimal

2. In algebra, a _____ is a function depending on n that associates a scalar, de, to every n×n square matrix A. The fundamental geometric meaning of a _____ is as the scale factor for measure when A is regarded as a linear transformation. _____s are important both in calculus, where they enter the substitution rule for several variables, and in multilinear algebra.

   a. Functional determinant
   b. Pfaffian
   c. Determinant
   d. 1-center problem

3. _____ is a form where m is the slope of the line and b is the y-intercept, which is the y-coordinate of the point where the line crosses the y axis. This can be seen by letting x = 0, which immediately gives y = b.

   a. Separable extension
   b. Commutative law
   c. Dynamical system
   d. Slope-intercept form

4. In mathematics, a _____ is a rectangular table of elements, which may be numbers or, more generally, any abstract quantities that can be added and multiplied. Matrices are used to describe linear equations, keep track of the coefficients of linear transformations and to record data that depend on multiple parameters. Matrices are described by the field of _____ theory.

   a. Compression
   b. Double counting
   c. Coherent
   d. Matrix

5. A _____ is an algebraic equation in which each term is either a constant or the product of a constant and a single variable. _____s can have one, two, three or more variables.

_____s occur with great regularity in applied mathematics.

   a. Difference of two squares
   b. Quadratic equation
   c. Quartic equation
   d. Linear equation

6. _____ generally conveys two primary meanings. The first is an imprecise sense of harmonious or aesthetically-pleasing proportionality and balance; such that it reflects beauty or perfection. The second meaning is a precise and well-defined concept of balance or 'patterned self-similarity' that can be demonstrated or proved according to the rules of a formal system: by geometry, through physics or otherwise.
   a. Molecular symmetry
   b. Tessellation
   c. Symmetry
   d. Symmetry breaking

7. In mathematics, the concept of a _____ tries to capture the intuitive idea of a geometrical one-dimensional and continuous object. A simple example is the circle. In everyday use of the term '_____', a straight line is not curved, but in mathematical parlance _____s include straight lines and line segments.
   a. Quadrifolium
   b. Negative pedal curve
   c. Curve
   d. Kappa curve

8. In mathematics, the _____ of a Euclidean space is a special point, usually denoted by the letter O, used as a fixed point of reference for the geometry of the surrounding space. In a Cartesian coordinate system, the _____ is the point where the axes of the system intersect. In Euclidean geometry, the _____ may be chosen freely as any convenient point of reference.
   a. OMAC
   b. Origin
   c. Autonomous system
   d. Interval

9. The _____ is the horizontal axis of a two- dimensional plot in the Cartesian coordinate system, that is typically pointed to the right. Also known as a right-handed coordinate system.

Chapter 1. Functions and Their Graphs

a. 1-center problem
b. 2-3 heap
c. 120-cell
d. X-axis

10. In reference to a 2D and 3D plane, the _____ is the vertical height of a 2D or 3D object.

a. 1-center problem
b. 120-cell
c. 2-3 heap
d. Y-axis

11. In abstract algebra, a field extension L /K is called _____ if every element of L is _____ over K. Field extensions which are not _____.

For example, the field extension R/Q, that is the field of real numbers as an extension of the field of rational numbers, is transcendental, while the field extensions C/R and Q

a. Echo
b. Algebraic
c. Identity
d. Ideal

12. A _____ is a simple shape of Euclidean geometry consisting of those points in a plane which are at a constant distance, called the radius, from a fixed point, called the center. A _____ with center A is sometimes denoted by the symbol A.

A chord of a _____ is a line segment whose two endpoints lie on the _____.

a. Circular segment
b. Malfatti circles
c. Circumcircle
d. Circle

13. _____, also sometimes known as standard form or as exponential notation, is a way of writing numbers that accommodates values too large or small to be conveniently written in standard decimal notation. _____ has a number of useful properties and is often favored by scientists, mathematicians and engineers, who work with such numbers.

Chapter 1. Functions and Their Graphs

In _____, numbers are written in the form:

$$a \times 10^b$$

a. Radix point
b. Scientific notation
c. 1-center problem
d. Leading zero

14. In mathematics, the _____s are an extension of the real numbers obtained by adjoining an imaginary unit, denoted i, which satisfies:

$$i^2 = -1.$$

Every _____ can be written in the form a + bi, where a and b are real numbers called the real part and the imaginary part of the _____, respectively.

_____s are a field, and thus have addition, subtraction, multiplication, and division operations. These operations extend the corresponding operations on real numbers, although with a number of additional elegant and useful properties, e.g., negative real numbers can be obtained by squaring _____s.

a. Real part
b. Complex number
c. 1-center problem
d. 120-cell

15. _____ is used to describe the steepness, incline, gradient, or grade of a straight line. A higher _____ value indicates a steeper incline. The _____ is defined as the ratio of the 'rise' divided by the 'run' between two points on a line, or in other words, the ratio of the altitude change to the horizontal distance between any two points on the line.
a. Slope
b. Cognitively Guided Instruction
c. Number line
d. Point plotting

16. In a graph theory, the _____ L

One of the earliest and most important theorems about _____s is due to Hassler Whitney, who proved that with one exceptional case the structure of G can be recovered completely from its _____.

a. Sparse graph
b. Line Graph
c. Vertex-transitive graph
d. Bivariegated graph

17. In mathematics, a _____ is, informally, an infinitely vast and infinitely thin sheet. _____s may be thought of as objects in some higher dimensional space, or they may be considered without any outside space, as in the setting of Euclidean geometry
    a. Group
    b. Blocking
    c. Bandwidth
    d. Plane

18. _____ is the change in total cost that arises when the quantity produced changes by one unit.
    a. Differential Algebra
    b. Notation
    c. Limiting
    d. Marginal cost

19. In economics, business, retail, and accounting, a _____ is the value of money that has been used up to produce something, and hence is not available for use anymore. In business, the _____ may be one of acquisition, in which case the amount of money expended to acquire it is counted as _____. In this case, money is the input that is gone in order to acquire the thing.
    a. 1-center problem
    b. 2-3 heap
    c. Cost
    d. 120-cell

20. The _____ expresses the fact that the difference in the y coordinate between two points on a line that is, y − y1 is proportional to the difference in the x coordinate that is, x − x1. The proportionality constant is m (the slope of the line.
    a. Cobb-Douglas
    b. Point-slope form
    c. Rubin Causal Model
    d. Square function

Chapter 1. Functions and Their Graphs

21. _____ is a method of curve fitting using linear polynomials. It is heavily employed in mathematics (particularly numerical analysis), and numerous applications including computer graphics. It is a simple form of interpolation.
    a. Polynomial interpolation
    b. Multivariate interpolation
    c. Monotone cubic interpolation
    d. Linear interpolation

22. _____ is a method of constructing new data points from a discrete set of known data points.
    a. Archimedes' use of infinitesimals
    b. Integration by substitution
    c. Interpolation
    d. Uniform convergence

23. A _____ of a curve is the envelope of a family of congruent circles centered on the curve. It generalises the concept of _____ lines.

    It is sometimes called the offset curve but the term 'offset' often refers also to translation.

    a. Cycloid
    b. Parallel
    c. Bifolium
    d. Cissoid

24. The existence and properties of _____ are the basis of Euclid's parallel postulate. _____ are two lines on the same plane that do not intersect even assuming that lines extend to infinity in either direction.
    a. Vertical translation
    b. Square wheel
    c. Spidron
    d. Parallel lines

25. In mathematics, the _____ is an approach to finding a particular solution to certain inhomogeneous ordinary differential equations and recurrence relations. It is closely related to the annihilator method, but instead of using a particular kind of differential operator in order to find the best possible form of the particular solution, a 'guess' is made as to the appropriate form, which is then tested by differentiating the resulting equation. In this sense, the _____ is less formal but more intuitive than the annihilator method.

Chapter 1. Functions and Their Graphs

a. Linear differential equation
b. Phase line
c. Method of undetermined coefficients
d. Differential algebraic equations

26. In accounting, _____ or carrying value is the value of an asset or according to its balance sheet account balance. For assets, the value is based on the original cost of the asset less any depreciation, amortization or impairment costs made against the asset. A company's _____ is its total assets minus intangible assets and liabilities.
    a. 120-cell
    b. Book value
    c. 1-center problem
    d. Depreciation

27. _____ is a term used in accounting, economics and finance to spread the cost of an asset over the span of several years.

In simple words we can say that _____ is the reduction in the value of an asset due to usage, passage of time, wear and tear, technological outdating or obsolescence, depletion or other such factors.

In accounting, _____ is a term used to describe any method of attributing the historical or purchase cost of an asset across its useful life, roughly corresponding to normal wear and tear.

   a. 120-cell
   b. Gross sales
   c. 1-center problem
   d. Depreciation

28. In mathematics, computing, linguistics and related subjects, an _____ is a sequence of finite instructions, often used for calculation and data processing. It is formally a type of effective method in which a list of well-defined instructions for completing a task will, when given an initial state, proceed through a well-defined series of successive states, eventually terminating in an end-state. The transition from one state to the next is not necessarily deterministic; some _____s, known as probabilistic _____s, incorporate randomness.
    a. Algorithm
    b. Approximate counting algorithm
    c. In-place algorithm
    d. Out-of-core

29. In mathematics, the _____ of a ring R, often denoted cha, is defined to be the smallest number of times one must add the ring's multiplicative identity element to itself to get the additive identity element; the ring is said to have _____ zero if this repeated sum never reaches the additive identity. That is, cha is the smallest positive number n such that

$$\underbrace{1 + \cdots + 1}_{n \text{ summands}} = 0$$

if such a number n exists, and 0 otherwise. The _____ may also be taken to be the exponent of the ring's additive group, that is, the smallest positive n such that

$$\underbrace{a + \cdots + a}_{n \text{ summands}} = 0$$

for every element a of the ring.

    a. Coherent
    b. Characteristic
    c. Disk
    d. Class

30. The mathematical concept of a _____ expresses the intuitive idea of deterministic dependence between two quantities, one of which is viewed as primary and the other as secondary. A _____ then is a way to associate a unique output for each input of a specified type, for example, a real number or an element of a given set.

    a. Grill
    b. Coherent
    c. Function
    d. Going up

31. In descriptive statistics, the _____ is the length of the smallest interval which contains all the data. It is calculated by subtracting the smallest observations from the greatest and provides an indication of statistical dispersion.

It is measured in the same units as the data.

    a. Kernel
    b. Range
    c. Bandwidth
    d. Class

Chapter 1. Functions and Their Graphs

32. In mathematics, especially in the area of abstract algebra known as ring theory, a _____ is a ring with 0 ≠ 1 such that ab = 0 implies that either a = 0 or b = 0. That is, it is a nontrivial ring without left or right zero divisors. A commutative _____ is called an integral _____.
    a. Left primitive ring
    b. Modular representation theory
    c. Simple ring
    d. Domain

33. _____ is the study of mathematical structures that are fundamentally discrete in the sense of not supporting or requiring the notion of continuity. Objects studied in _____ are largely countable sets such as integers, finite graphs, and formal languages.

    _____ has become popular in recent decades because of its applications to computer science.

    a. Partial equivalence relation
    b. Discrete mathematics
    c. Pooling design
    d. Dual graph

34. _____ and independent variables refer to values that change in relationship to each other. The _____ are those that are observed to change in response to the independent variables. The independent variables are those that are deliberately manipulated to invoke a change in the _____.
    a. Round robin test
    b. Steiner system
    c. Yates analysis
    d. Dependent variables

35. Dependent variables and _____ refer to values that change in relationship to each other. The dependent variables are those that are observed to change in response to the _____. The _____ are those that are deliberately manipulated to invoke a change in the dependent variables.
    a. Operational confound
    b. Experimental design diagram
    c. Independent variables
    d. One-factor-at-a-time method

36. In mathematics, a _____ is a function whose definition is dependent on the value of the independent variable. Mathematically, a real-valued function f of a real variable x is a relationship whose definition is given differently on disjoint subsets of its domain

The word piecewise is also used to describe any property of a _____ that holds for each piece but may not hold for the whole domain of the function.

a. High-dimensional model representation
b. Glide reflection
c. Surjective
d. Piecewise-defined function

37. In mathematics, a _____ is the end result of a division problem. It can also be expressed as the number of times the divisor divides into the dividend.
a. Limiting
b. Marginal cost
c. Notation
d. Quotient

38. In mathematics, _____ and undefined are used to explain whether or not expressions have meaningful, sensible, and unambiguous values. Not all branches of mathematics come to the same conclusion.

The following expressions are undefined in all contexts, but remarks in the analysis section may apply.

a. Toy model
b. LHS
c. Defined
d. Plugging in

39. _____ is the study of terms and their use. Terms are words and compound words that are used in specific contexts. Not to be confused with 'terms' in colloquial usages, the shortened form of technical terms which are defined within a discipline or specialty field.
a. 120-cell
b. Terminology
c. 2-3 heap
d. 1-center problem

40. In mathematics, a _____ is a function whose values do not vary and thus are constant. For example, if we have the function f→ B is a _____ if f

a. Squeeze mapping
b. Linear operator
c. Point reflection
d. Constant function

41. In calculus, a function f defined on a subset of the real numbers with real values is called monotonic (also monotonically increasing or non-_____), if for all x and y such that x ≤ y one has f(x) ≤ f(y), so f preserves the order. In layman's terms, the sign of the slope is always positive (the curve tending upwards) or zero (i.e., non-_____, or asymptotic, or depicted as a horizontal, flat line) Likewise, a function is called monotonically _____ (non-increasing) if, whenever x ≤ y, then f(x) ≥ f(y), so it reverses the order.
    a. Dual pair
    b. Circular convolution
    c. Decreasing
    d. Tensor product of Hilbert spaces

42. A real-valued function f defined on the real line is said to have a _____ point at the point x∗, if there exists some ε > 0, such that f when x − x∗ < ε.
    a. Binomial series
    b. Calculus controversy
    c. Hyperbolic angle
    d. Local maximum

43. In mathematics, even functions and _____s are functions which satisfy particular symmetry relations, with respect to taking additive inverses. They are important in many areas of mathematical analysis, especially the theory of power series and Fourier series. They are named for the parity of the powers of the power functions which satisfy each condition: the function f(x) = x^n is an even function if n is an even integer, and it is an _____ if n is an odd integer.
    a. A Mathematical Theory of Communication
    b. A posteriori
    c. Odd function
    d. A chemical equation

Chapter 1. Functions and Their Graphs

44. In mathematics, the term _____ has several different important meanings:

- An _____ is an equality that remains true regardless of the values of any variables that appear within it, to distinguish it from an equality which is true under more particular conditions. For this, the 'triple bar' symbol ≡ is sometimes used.
- In algebra, an _____ or _____ element of a set S with a binary operation Â· is an element e that, when combined with any element x of S, produces that same x. That is, eÂ·x = xÂ·e = x for all x in S.
    - The _____ function from a set S to itself, often denoted id or id_S, s the function such that i = x for all x in S. This function serves as the _____ element in the set of all functions from S to itself with respect to function composition.
    - In linear algebra, the _____ matrix of size n is the n-by-n square matrix with ones on the main diagonal and zeros elsewhere. This matrix serves as the _____ with respect to matrix multiplication.

A common example of the first meaning is the trigonometric _____

$$\sin^2 \theta + \cos^2 \theta = 1$$

which is true for all real values of θ, as opposed to

$$\cos \theta = 1,$$

which is true only for some values of θ, not all. For example, the latter equation is true when $\theta = 0$, false when $\theta = 2$

The concepts of 'additive _____' and 'multiplicative _____' are central to the Peano axioms. The number 0 is the 'additive _____' for integers, real numbers, and complex numbers. For the real numbers, for all $a \in \mathbb{R}$,

$$0 + a = a,$$

$$a + 0 = a, \text{ and}$$

$$0 + 0 = 0.$$

Similarly, The number 1 is the 'multiplicative _____' for integers, real numbers, and complex numbers.

a. Identity
b. Intersection
c. ARIA
d. Action

Chapter 1. Functions and Their Graphs

45. An _____ is a function that does not have any effect: it always returns the same value that was used as its argument.

   a. Angle bisector
   b. Algebra
   c. Inverse function
   d. Identity function

46. In mathematics, a _____ is a function of the form

   $f3 + bx^2 + cx + d$,

   where a is nonzero; or in other words, a polynomial of degree three. The derivative of a _____ is a quadratic function. The integral of a _____ is a quartic function.

   a. Quartic equation
   b. Quadratic equation
   c. Linear equation
   d. Cubic function

47. In mathematics, the multiplicative inverse of a number x, denoted 1/x or x^{-1}, is the number which, when multiplied by x, yields 1. The multiplicative inverse of x is also called the _____ of x.

   a. 2-3 heap
   b. 1-center problem
   c. Reciprocal
   d. 120-cell

48. A _____ usually denotes a function which maps a matrix to a matrix.

   There are several techniques for lifting a real function to a square _____ such that interesting properties are maintained. All of the following techniques yield the same _____, but the domains on which the function are defined may differ.

   a. Nullity theorem
   b. Minimal polynomial
   c. Matrix exponential
   d. Matrix function

Chapter 1. Functions and Their Graphs

49. In vascular plants, the _____ is the organ of a plant body that typically lies below the surface of the soil. This is not always the case, however, since a _____ can also be aerial (that is, growing above the ground) or aerating (that is, growing up above the ground or especially above water.) Furthermore, a stem normally occurring below ground is not exceptional either
    a. Root
    b. 1-center problem
    c. 2-3 heap
    d. 120-cell

50. In mathematics, a _____ of a number x is a number r such that $r^2 = x$, or, in other words, a number r whose square is x. Every non-negative real number x has a unique non-negative _____, called the principal _____, which is denoted with a radical symbol as $\sqrt{x}$, or, using exponent notation, as $x^{1/2}$. For example, the principal _____ of 9 is 3, denoted $\sqrt{9} = 3$, because $3^2 = 3 \times 3 = 9$.
    a. Hyperbolic functions
    b. Multiplicative inverse
    c. Double exponential
    d. Square root

51. The _____ are the set of numbers consisting of the natural numbers including 0 and their negatives. They are numbers that can be written without a fractional or decimal component, and fall within the set {... −2, −1, 0, 1, 2, ...}.
    a. A posteriori
    b. A chemical equation
    c. A Mathematical Theory of Communication
    d. Integers

52. In statistics, the _____ problem occurs when one considers a set of statistical inferences simultaneously. Errors in inference, including confidence intervals that fail to include their corresponding population parameters are more likely when one considers the family as a whole.

    The term 'comparisons' in _____ typically refers to comparisons of two groups, such as treatment versus control.

    a. Familywise error rate
    b. Cross-validation
    c. Closed testing procedure
    d. Multiple comparisons

Chapter 1. Functions and Their Graphs

53. In mathematics, an arithmetic progression or _____ is a sequence of numbers such that the difference of any two successive members of the sequence is a constant. For instance, the sequence 3, 5, 7, 9, 11, 13... is an arithmetic progression with common difference 2.
    a. Eisenstein series
    b. Edgeworth series
    c. Alternating series test
    d. Arithmetic sequence

54. In combinatorial mathematics, a _____ is an un-ordered collection of distinct elements, usually of a prescribed size and taken from a given set. Given such a set S, a _____ of elements of S is just a subset of S, where as always forsets the order of the elements is not taken into account. Also, as always forsets, no elements can be repeated more than once in a _____; this is often referred to as a 'collection without repetition'.
    a. Fill-in
    b. Sparsity
    c. Combination
    d. Heawood number

55. In mathematics, the _____ of a number n is the number that, when added to n, yields zero. The _____ of n is denoted −n. For example, 7 is −7, because 7 + (−7) = 0, and the _____ of −0.3 is 0.3, because −0.3 + 0.3 = 0.
    a. Algebraic structure
    b. Arity
    c. Associativity
    d. Additive inverse

56. An _____ is a function which does the reverse of a given function.
    a. Empty function
    b. A Mathematical Theory of Communication
    c. Empty set
    d. Inverse function

57. In mathematics, the _____ is a test used to determine if a function is injective, surjective or bijective.

Suppose there is a function f : X → Y with a graph., and you have a horizontal line of X x Y :
$y_0 \in Y, \{(x, y_0) : x \in X\} = (X \times y_0)$.

- If the function is injective, then it can be visualized as one whose graph is never intersected by any horizontal line more than once.
- Iff f is surjective any horizontal line will intersect the graph at least at one point
- If f is bijective any horizontal line will intersect the graph at exactly one point.

This test is also used to find whether or not the inverse of the function is indeed a function as well. This is due to the reflective properties of the function over y=x.

a. Subset
b. Multiset
c. Disjoint sets
d. Horizontal Line Test

58. An injective function is called an injection, and is also said to be a _____ (not to be confused with one-to-one correspondence, i.e. a bijective function.)

A function f that is not injective is sometimes called many-to-one. (However, this terminology is also sometimes used to mean 'single-valued', i.e. each argument is mapped to at most one value.)

a. A chemical equation
b. A posteriori
c. One-to-one function
d. A Mathematical Theory of Communication

59. _____ is a special mathematical relationship between two quantities. Two quantities are called proportional if they vary in such a way that one of the quantities is a constant multiple of the other, or equivalently if they have a constant ratio.
a. Discontinuity
b. Depth
c. Compression
d. Proportionality

60. In mathematics, two quantities are called _____ if they vary in such a way that one of the quantities is a constant multiple of the other, or equivalently if they have a constant ratio.

a. Proportional
b. 2-3 heap
c. 1-center problem
d. 120-cell

61. It is sometimes mistakenly thought that one context in which uncorrelatedness implies independence is when the random variables involved are normally distributed. Here are the facts:

- Suppose two random variables X and Y are _____ normally distributed. That is the same as saying that the random vector has a multivariate normal distribution. It means that the joint probability distribution of X and Y is such that for any two constant scalars a and b, the random variable aX + bY is normally distributed. In that case if X and Y are uncorrelated.

- But it is possible for two random variables X and Y to be so distributed _____ that each one alone is normally distributed, and they are uncorrelated, but they are not independent. Examples appear below.

Suppose X has a normal distribution with expected value 0 and variance 1.

a. Context-sensitive language
b. Continuous wavelet
c. Convex set
d. Jointly

62. In mathematics, a _____ is a constant multiplicative factor of a certain object. For example, in the expression $9x^2$, the _____ of x^2 is 9.

The object can be such things as a variable, a vector, a function, etc.

a. Coefficient
b. Multivariate division algorithm
c. Fibonacci polynomials
d. Stability radius

63. In probability theory and statistics, _____ indicates the strength and direction of a linear relationship between two random variables. That is in contrast with the usage of the term in colloquial speech, denoting any relationship, not necessarily linear. In general statistical usage, _____ or co-relation refers to the departure of two random variables from independence.

18   *Chapter 1. Functions and Their Graphs*

    a. Summary statistics
    b. Sample size
    c. Random variables
    d. Correlation

64. The method of _____ or ordinary _____ is used to solve overdetermined systems. _____ is often applied in statistical contexts, particularly regression analysis.

_____ can be interpreted as a method of fitting data.

    a. Rata Die
    b. Non-linear least squares
    c. System equivalence
    d. Least squares

65. In elementary algebra, a _____ is a polynomial with two terms: the sum of two monomials. It is the simplest kind of polynomial except for a monomial.

The _____ $a^2 - b^2$ can be factored as the product of two other _____s:

    $a^2 - b^2$.

The product of a pair of linear _____s $a x + b$ and $c x + d$ is:

    $2 + x + bd$.

A _____ raised to the nth power, represented as

    n

can be expanded by means of the _____ theorem or, equivalently, using Pascal's triangle.

    a. Real structure
    b. Binomial
    c. Rational root theorem
    d. Cylindrical algebraic decomposition

66. The _____ fallacy is an informal fallacy. It ascribes cause where none exists. The flaw is failing to account for natural fluctuations.

Chapter 1. Functions and Their Graphs

a. Degrees of freedom
b. Depth
c. Differential
d. Regression

67. In propositional logic, contraposition is a logical relationship between two statements of material implication. A proposition Q is materially implicated by a proposition P when the following relationship holds:

$$(P \rightarrow Q)$$

In vernacular terms, this states 'If P then Q', or, 'If Socrates is a man then Socrates is human.' In a conditional such as this, P is called the antecedent and Q the consequent. One statement is the _____ of the other just when its antecedent is the negated consequent of the other, and vice-versa.

a. Control chart
b. Continuous signal
c. Contour map
d. Contrapositive

68. In logic and mathematics, _____ or not is an operation on logical values, for example, the logical value of a proposition, that sends true to false and false to true. Intuitively, the _____ of a proposition holds exactly when that proposition does not hold. In grammar, nor is an adverb which acts as a coordinating conjunction.

a. Syntax
b. Sentence diagram
c. 1-center problem
d. Negation

Chapter 2. Polynomial and Rational Functions

1. The mathematical concept of a _____ expresses the intuitive idea of deterministic dependence between two quantities, one of which is viewed as primary and the other as secondary. A _____ then is a way to associate a unique output for each input of a specified type, for example, a real number or an element of a given set.
   a. Function
   b. Going up
   c. Coherent
   d. Grill

2. In mathematics, the _____ is a conic section, the intersection of a right circular conical surface and a plane parallel to a generating straight line of that surface. Given a point and a line that lie in a plane, the locus of points in that plane that are equidistant to them is a _____.

   A particular case arises when the plane is tangent to the conical surface of a circle.

   a. Matrix representation of conic sections
   b. Parabola
   c. Dandelin sphere
   d. Directrix

3. In mathematics, a _____ is an expression constructed from variables and constants, using the operations of addition, subtraction, multiplication, and constant non-negative whole number exponents. For example, $x^2 - 4x + 7$ is a _____, but $x^2 - 4/x + 7x^{3/2}$ is not, because its second term involves division by the variable x and also because its third term contains an exponent that is not a whole number.

   _____s are one of the most important concepts in algebra and throughout mathematics and science.

   a. Semifield
   b. Polynomial
   c. Coimage
   d. Group extension

4. A _____, in mathematics, is a polynomial function of the form $f(x) = ax^2 + bx + c$, where $a \neq 0$. The graph of a _____ is a parabola whose major axis is parallel to the y-axis.

   The expression $ax^2 + bx + c$ in the definition of a _____ is a polynomial of degree 2 or a 2nd degree polynomial, because the highest exponent of x is 2.

Chapter 2. Polynomial and Rational Functions

a. Quadratic function
b. Laguerre polynomials
c. Discriminant
d. Multivariate division algorithm

5. _____ generally conveys two primary meanings. The first is an imprecise sense of harmonious or aesthetically-pleasing proportionality and balance; such that it reflects beauty or perfection. The second meaning is a precise and well-defined concept of balance or 'patterned self-similarity' that can be demonstrated or proved according to the rules of a formal system: by geometry, through physics or otherwise.
   a. Molecular symmetry
   b. Symmetry breaking
   c. Tessellation
   d. Symmetry

6. In geometry, a _____ is a special kind of point, usually a corner of a polygon, polyhedron, or higher dimensional polytope. In the geometry of curves a _____ is a point of where the first derivative of curvature is zero. In graph theory, a _____ is the fundamental unit out of which graphs are formed
   a. Dini
   b. Crib
   c. Duality
   d. Vertex

7. In geometry and trigonometry, an _____ is the figure formed by two rays sharing a common endpoint, called the vertex of the _____. The magnitude of the _____ is the 'amount of rotation' that separates the two rays, and can be measured by considering the length of circular arc swept out when one ray is rotated about the vertex to coincide with the other. Where there is no possibility of confusion, the term '_____' is used interchangeably for both the geometric configuration itself and for its angular magnitude.
   a. A chemical equation
   b. A Mathematical Theory of Communication
   c. A posteriori
   d. Angle

8. _____, also sometimes known as standard form or as exponential notation, is a way of writing numbers that accommodates values too large or small to be conveniently written in standard decimal notation. _____ has a number of useful properties and is often favored by scientists, mathematicians and engineers, who work with such numbers.

In _____, numbers are written in the form:

$$a \times 10^b$$

a. Radix point
b. 1-center problem
c. Leading zero
d. Scientific notation

9. In mathematics, the _____s are an extension of the real numbers obtained by adjoining an imaginary unit, denoted i, which satisfies:

$$i^2 = -1.$$

Every _____ can be written in the form a + bi, where a and b are real numbers called the real part and the imaginary part of the _____, respectively.

_____s are a field, and thus have addition, subtraction, multiplication, and division operations. These operations extend the corresponding operations on real numbers, although with a number of additional elegant and useful properties, e.g., negative real numbers can be obtained by squaring _____s.

a. 1-center problem
b. Real part
c. Complex number
d. 120-cell

10. In probability theory, a probability distribution is called _____ if its cumulative distribution function is _____. That is equivalent to saying that for random variables X with the distribution in question, Pr[X = a] = 0 for all real numbers a. If the distribution of X is _____ then X is called a _____ random variable.

a. Conull set
b. Continuous phase modulation
c. Continuous
d. Concatenated codes

11. In mathematics, a _____ is a function for which, intuitively, small changes in the input result in small changes in the output. Otherwise, a function is said to be discontinuous. A _____ with a continuous inverse function is called bicontinuous.

Chapter 2. Polynomial and Rational Functions

a. Contraction mapping
b. Charles's Law
c. Beth numbers
d. Continuous function

12. In mathematics, a _____ is a constant multiplicative factor of a certain object. For example, in the expression $9x^2$, the _____ of x^2 is 9.

The object can be such things as a variable, a vector, a function, etc.

a. Stability radius
b. Fibonacci polynomials
c. Coefficient
d. Multivariate division algorithm

13. In mathematics, a _____ is a set of real numbers with the property that any number that lies between two numbers in the set is also included in the set. For example, the set of all numbers x satisfying $0 \leq x \leq 1$ is an _____ which contains 0 and 1, as well as all numbers between them. Other examples of _____s are the set of all real numbers $\mathbb{R}$, the set of all positive real numbers, and the empty set.

a. Order
b. Annihilator
c. Ideal
d. Interval

14. In mathematics, the _____ system is a two-dimensional coordinate system in which each point on a plane is determined by an angle and a distance. The _____ system is especially useful in situations where the relationship between two points is most easily expressed in terms of angles and distance; in the more familiar Cartesian or rectangular coordinate system, such a relationship can only be found through trigonometric formulation.

As the coordinate system is two-dimensional, each point is determined by two _____s: the radial coordinate and the angular coordinate.

a. Sir Isaac Newton
b. Vampire
c. Sequence alignment
d. Polar coordinate

15. In mathematical analysis, the _____ states that for each value between the least upper bound and greatest lower bound of the image of a continuous function there is a corresponding value in its domain mapping to the original. _____

- Version I. The _____ states the following: If the function y = f∈ [a, b] such that f

- Version II. Suppose that I is an interval [a, b] in the real numbers R and that f : I → R is a continuous function. Then the image set f

    f⊇ [f or f(I) ⊇ [f(b), f(a)].

It is frequently stated in the following equivalent form: Suppose that f : [a, b] → R is continuous and that u is a real number satisfying f(a) < u < f(b) or f(a) > u > f(b.) Then for some c ∈ [a, b], f(c) = u.

This captures an intuitive property of continuous functions: given f continuous on [1, 2], if f(1) = 3 and f(2) = 5 then f must take the value 4 somewhere between 1 and 2.

a. Intermediate Value Theorem
b. Equicontinuous
c. Uniformly continuous
d. A Mathematical Theory of Communication

16. In mathematics, a _____ is a statement that can be proved on the basis of explicitly stated or previously agreed assumptions.
a. Boolean function
b. Disjunction introduction
c. Logical value
d. Theorem

17. In mathematics, computing, linguistics and related subjects, an _____ is a sequence of finite instructions, often used for calculation and data processing. It is formally a type of effective method in which a list of well-defined instructions for completing a task will, when given an initial state, proceed through a well-defined series of successive states, eventually terminating in an end-state. The transition from one state to the next is not necessarily deterministic; some _____s, known as probabilistic _____s, incorporate randomness.
a. Algorithm
b. Approximate counting algorithm
c. Out-of-core
d. In-place algorithm

Chapter 2. Polynomial and Rational Functions 25

18. In mathematics, and in particular in abstract algebra, distributivity is a property of binary operations that generalises the _____ law from elementary algebra.
    a. Closure with a twist
    b. General linear group
    c. Permutation
    d. Distributive

19. In mathematics, the _____ of a complex number z, is the second element of the ordered pair of real numbers representing z,. It is denoted by Im or $\Im\{z\}$, where $\Im$ is a capital I in the Fraktur typeface. The complex function which maps z to the _____ of z is not holomorphic.
    a. A Mathematical Theory of Communication
    b. A chemical equation
    c. A posteriori
    d. Imaginary part

20. In mathematics, the _____ of a complex number z, is the first element of the ordered pair of real numbers representing z. It is denoted by Re{z} or $\Re\{z\}$, where $\Re$ is a capital R in the Fraktur typeface. The complex function which maps z to the _____ of z is not holomorphic.
    a. Real part
    b. Complex number
    c. 120-cell
    d. 1-center problem

21. In mathematics the _____ of a set which is equipped with the operation of addition is an element which, when added to any element x in the set, yields x. One of the most familiar additive identities is the number 0 from elementary mathematics, but additive identities occur in other mathematical structures where addition is defined, such as in groups and rings.

- The _____ familiar from elementary mathematics is zero, denoted 0. For example,

    5 + 0 = 5 = 0 + 5.

- In the natural numbers N and all of its supersets, the _____ is 0. Thus for any one of these numbers n,

    n + 0 = n = 0 + n.

Let N be a set which is closed under the operation of addition, denoted +. An _____ for N is any element e such that for any element n in N,

e + n = n = n + e.

a. Unique factorization domain
b. Algebraically independent
c. Unit ring
d. Additive identity

22. In mathematics, the term _____ has several different important meanings:

- An _____ is an equality that remains true regardless of the values of any variables that appear within it, to distinguish it from an equality which is true under more particular conditions. For this, the 'triple bar' symbol ≡ is sometimes used.
- In algebra, an _____ or _____ element of a set S with a binary operation Â· is an element e that, when combined with any element x of S, produces that same x. That is, eÂ·x = xÂ·e = x for all x in S.
  - The _____ function from a set S to itself, often denoted id or id_S, s the function such that i = x for all x in S. This function serves as the _____ element in the set of all functions from S to itself with respect to function composition.
  - In linear algebra, the _____ matrix of size n is the n-by-n square matrix with ones on the main diagonal and zeros elsewhere. This matrix serves as the _____ with respect to matrix multiplication.

A common example of the first meaning is the trigonometric _____

$$\sin^2 \theta + \cos^2 \theta = 1$$

which is true for all real values of θ, as opposed to

$$\cos \theta = 1,$$

which is true only for some values of θ, not all. For example, the latter equation is true when $\theta = 0$, false when $\theta = 2$

The concepts of 'additive _____' and 'multiplicative _____' are central to the Peano axioms. The number 0 is the 'additive _____' for integers, real numbers, and complex numbers. For the real numbers, for all $a \in \mathbb{R}$,

$$0 + a = a,$$

$$a + 0 = a, \text{ and}$$

$$0 + 0 = 0.$$

Similarly, The number 1 is the 'multiplicative _____' for integers, real numbers, and complex numbers.

Chapter 2. Polynomial and Rational Functions

   a. Action
   b. Identity
   c. ARIA
   d. Intersection

23. In mathematics, the _____ of a number n is the number that, when added to n, yields zero. The _____ of n is denoted −n. For example, 7 is −7, because 7 + (−7) = 0, and the _____ of −0.3 is 0.3, because −0.3 + 0.3 = 0.
   a. Algebraic structure
   b. Additive inverse
   c. Associativity
   d. Arity

24. In mathematics, _____ is a property that a binary operation can have. It means that, within an expression containing two or more of the same associative operators in a row, the order that the operations are performed does not matter as long as the sequence of the operands is not changed. That is, rearranging the parentheses in such an expression will not change its value.
   a. Idempotence
   b. Unital
   c. Algebraically closed
   d. Associativity

25. The _____ is a rule which states that when you add or multiply numbers, changing the order doesn't change the result.
   a. Semigroupoid
   b. Coimage
   c. Conditional event algebra
   d. Commutative law

26. _____ is the mathematical operation of scaling one number by another. It is one of the four basic operations in elementary arithmetic.

_____ is defined for whole numbers in terms of repeated addition; for example, 4 multiplied by 3 can be calculated by adding 3 copies of 4 together:

$$4 + 4 + 4 = 12.$$

_____ of rational numbers and real numbers is defined by systematic generalization of this basic idea.

a. Multiplication
b. Highest common factor
c. The number 0 is even.
d. Least common multiple

27. In mathematics, the _____ of a complex number is given by changing the sign of the imaginary part. Thus, the conjugate of the complex number

$$z = a + ib$$

(where a and b are real numbers) is

$$\bar{z} = a - ib.$$

The _____ is also very commonly denoted by z*. Here $\bar{z}$ is chosen to avoid confusion with the notation for the conjugate transpose of a matrix (which can be thought of as a generalization of complex conjugation.)

a. Real part
b. 120-cell
c. 1-center problem
d. Complex conjugate

28. In algebra, a _____ of an element in a quadratic extension field of a field K is its image under the unique non-identity automorphism of the extended field that fixes K. If the extension is generated by a square root of an element r of K, then the _____ of $a + b\sqrt{r}$ is $a - b\sqrt{r}$ for $a, b \in K$, and in particular in the case of the field C of complex numbers as an extension of the field R of real numbers, the complex _____ of a + bi is a − bi.

Forming the sum or product of any element of the extension field with its _____ always gives an element of K.

a. Trinomial
b. Relation algebra
c. Real structure
d. Conjugate

29. In mathematics, a _____ is a rectangular table of elements, which may be numbers or, more generally, any abstract quantities that can be added and multiplied. Matrices are used to describe linear equations, keep track of the coefficients of linear transformations and to record data that depend on multiple parameters. Matrices are described by the field of _____ theory.

Chapter 2. Polynomial and Rational Functions

a. Double counting
b. Matrix
c. Coherent
d. Compression

30. In vascular plants, the _____ is the organ of a plant body that typically lies below the surface of the soil. This is not always the case, however, since a _____ can also be aerial (that is, growing above the ground) or aerating (that is, growing up above the ground or especially above water.) Furthermore, a stem normally occurring below ground is not exceptional either
    a. 120-cell
    b. 2-3 heap
    c. 1-center problem
    d. Root

31. In mathematics, a _____ of a number x is a number r such that r^2 = x, or, in other words, a number r whose square is x. Every non-negative real number x has a unique non-negative _____, called the principal _____, which is denoted with a radical symbol as $\sqrt{x}$, or, using exponent notation, as $x^{1/2}$. For example, the principal _____ of 9 is 3, denoted $\sqrt{9}$ = 3, because 3^2 = 3 × 3 = 9.
    a. Multiplicative inverse
    b. Double exponential
    c. Hyperbolic functions
    d. Square root

32. In mathematics, an _____ is a theorem with a statement beginning 'there exis ..' y, ... there exis ...'. That is, in more formal terms of symbolic logic, it is a theorem with a statement involving the existential quantifier.
    a. A chemical equation
    b. A Mathematical Theory of Communication
    c. A posteriori
    d. Existence theorem

33. In mathematics, the _____ states that every non-constant single-variable polynomial with complex coefficients has at least one complex root. Equivalently, the field of complex numbers is algebraically closed.

Sometimes, this theorem is stated as: every non-zero single-variable polynomial, with complex coefficients, has exactly as many complex roots as its degree, if each root is counted up to its multiplicity.

a. Closure with a twist
b. Distributive
c. Fundamental Theorem of Algebra
d. Near-semiring

34. In mathematics, a _____ is a number which can be expressed as a ratio of two integers. Non-integer _____s are usually written as the vulgar fraction $\frac{a}{b}$, where b is not zero. a is called the numerator, and b the denominator.
a. Minkowski distance
b. Rational number
c. Pre-algebra
d. Tally marks

35. In mathematics, the _____ of a non-negative integer n, denoted by n!, is the product of all positive integers less than or equal to n. For example,

$$5! = 1 \times 2 \times 3 \times 4 \times 5 = 120$$

and
$$6! = 1 \times 2 \times 3 \times 4 \times 5 \times 6 = 720$$

The notation n! was introduced by Christian Kramp in 1808.

The _____ function is formally defined by

$$n! = \prod_{k=1}^{n} k \qquad \forall n \in \mathbb{N}.$$

The above definition incorporates the instance

$$0! = 1$$

as an instance of the fact that the product of no numbers at all is 1.

a. Symbolic combinatorics
b. Partition of a set
c. Factorial
d. Plane partition

36. In mathematics, a _____ is a natural number which has exactly two distinct natural number divisors: 1 and itself. An infinitude of _____s exists, as demonstrated by Euclid around 300 BC. The first twenty-five _____s are:

2, 3, 5, 7, 11, 13, 17, 19, 23, 29, 31, 37, 41, 43, 47, 53, 59, 61, 67, 71, 73, 79, 83, 89, 97.

a. Perrin number
b. Highly composite number
c. Pronic number
d. Prime number

37. In number theory, the _____s of a positive integer are the prime numbers that divide into that integer exactly, without leaving a remainder. The process of finding these numbers is called integer factorization, or prime factorization.

For a _____ p of n, the multiplicity of p is the largest exponent a for which p^a divides n.

a. Gigantic prime
b. Prime factor
c. Wieferich pair
d. Cunningham chain

38. In mathematics, especially in order theory, an upper bound of a subset S of some partially ordered set is an element of P which is greater than or equal to every element of S. The term _____ is defined dually as an element of P which is lesser than or equal to every element of S. A set with an upper bound is said to be bounded from above by that bound, a set with a _____ is said to be bounded from below by that bound.

a. Partially ordered set
b. Monomial order
c. Cofinality
d. Lower Bound

39. In mathematics, especially in order theory, an _____ of a subset S of some partially ordered set is an element of P which is greater than or equal to every element of S. The term lower bound is defined dually as an element of P which is lesser than or equal to every element of S. A set with an _____ is said to be bounded from above by that bound, a set with a lower bound is said to be bounded from below by that bound.

a. Upper bound
b. Order isomorphism
c. Infinite descending chain
d. Order-embedding

40. In mathematics, a _____ is any function which can be written as the ratio of two polynomial functions. _____ of degree 2 :
$$y = \frac{x^2 - 3x - 2}{x^2 - 4}$$

In the case of one variable, x, a _____ is a function of the form

$$f(x) = \frac{P(x)}{Q(x)}$$

where P and Q are polynomial function in x and Q is not the zero polynomial. The domain of f is the set of all points x for which the denominator Q

a. 1-center problem
b. Legendre rational functions
c. 120-cell
d. Rational function

41. In mathematics, especially in the area of abstract algebra known as ring theory, a _____ is a ring with 0 ≠ 1 such that ab = 0 implies that either a = 0 or b = 0. That is, it is a nontrivial ring without left or right zero divisors. A commutative _____ is called an integral _____.

a. Modular representation theory
b. Domain
c. Left primitive ring
d. Simple ring

42. An _____ of a real-valued function y = f(x) is a curve which describes the behavior of f as either x or y tends to infinity.

In other words, as one moves along the graph of f(x) in some direction, the distance between it and the _____ eventually becomes smaller than any distance that one may specify.

If a curve A has the curve B as an _____, one says that A is asymptotic to B. Similarly B is asymptotic to A, so A and B are called asymptotic.

a. Infinite product
b. Asymptote
c. Improper integral
d. Isoperimetric dimension

43. Suppose f is a function. Then the line y = a is a _____ for f if

$$\lim_{x \to \infty} f(x) = a \text{ or } \lim_{x \to -\infty} f(x) = a.$$

Intuitively, this means that f(x) can be made as close as desired to a by making x big enough. How big is big enough depends on how close one wishes to make f(x) to a.

a. 2-3 heap
b. Horizontal asymptote
c. 120-cell
d. 1-center problem

44. When a linear asymptote is not parallel to the x- or y-axis, it is called either an oblique asymptote or equivalently a _____. The function f(x) is asymptotic to y = mx + b if

$$\lim_{x \to \infty} f(x) - (mx + b) = 0 \text{ or } \lim_{x \to -\infty} f(x) - (mx + b) = 0$$

Note that y = mx + b is never a vertical asymptote, but can be a horizontal asymptote if m=0 (in which case it is not an oblique asymptote.)

An example is $f(x)=(x^2-1)/x$ which has an oblique asymptote of y=x (m=1, b=0) as seen in the limit

$$\lim_{x \to \infty} f(x) - x$$
$$= \lim_{x \to \infty} \frac{x^2 - 1}{x} - x$$
$$= \lim_{x \to \infty} (x - 1/x) - x$$
$$= \lim_{x \to \infty} -1/x = 0$$

34 Chapter 2. Polynomial and Rational Functions

Computationally identifying an oblique asymptote can be more difficult than a horizontal or vertical asymptote, in particular because the m and b might not be known.

a. Slant asymptote
b. 1-center problem
c. 2-3 heap
d. 120-cell

45. A _____ is generally 'a rough or fragmented geometric shape that can be split into parts, each of which is a reduced-size copy of the whole,' a property called self-similarity. The term was coined by Benoît Mandelbrot in 1975 and was derived from the Latin fractus meaning 'broken' or 'fractured.' A mathematical _____ is based on an equation that undergoes iteration, a form of feedback based on recursion.

A _____ often has the following features:

- It has a fine structure at arbitrarily small scales.
- It is too irregular to be easily described in traditional Euclidean geometric language.
- It is self-similar.
- It has a Hausdorff dimension which is greater than its topological dimension.
- It has a simple and recursive definition.

Because they appear similar at all levels of magnification, _____s are often considered to be infinitely complex. Natural objects that approximate _____s to a degree include clouds, mountain ranges, lightning bolts, coastlines, and snow flakes.

a. Logical disjunction
b. Cube
c. Zero-point energy
d. Fractal

46. In algebra, the _____ decomposition or _____ expansion is used to reduce the degree of either the numerator or the denominator of a rational function. The outcome of _____ expansion expresses that function as a sum of fractions, where:

- the denominator of each term is a power of an irreducible polynomial and
- the numerator is a polynomial of smaller degree than that irreducible polynomial.

See _____s in integration for an account of their use in finding antiderivatives. They are also used in calculating the inverse of transforms; such as the Laplace transform, or the Z-transform.

The basic idea behind _____s is to work backwards to separate a function.

a. Continuant
b. Concept algebra
c. Real structure
d. Partial fraction

47. In elementary algebra, a _____ is a polynomial with two terms: the sum of two monomials. It is the simplest kind of polynomial except for a monomial.

The _____ $a^2 - b^2$ can be factored as the product of two other _____s:

$a^2 - b^2$.

The product of a pair of linear _____s $ax + b$ and $cx + d$ is:

$2 + x + bd$.

A _____ raised to the nth power, represented as

n

can be expanded by means of the _____ theorem or, equivalently, using Pascal's triangle.

a. Rational root theorem
b. Cylindrical algebraic decomposition
c. Real structure
d. Binomial

1. In abstract algebra, a field extension L /K is called _____ if every element of L is _____ over K. Field extensions which are not _____.

For example, the field extension R/Q, that is the field of real numbers as an extension of the field of rational numbers, is transcendental, while the field extensions C/R and Q

   a. Echo
   b. Identity
   c. Ideal
   d. Algebraic

2. In mathematics, an _____ is informally a function which satisfies a polynomial equation whose coefficients are themselves polynomials. For example, an _____ in one variable x is a solution y for an equation

$$a_n(x)y^n + a_{n-1}(x)y^{n-1} + \cdots + a_0(x) = 0$$

where the coefficients a_i

   a. Algebraic function
   b. Alternatization
   c. Algebraic signal processing
   d. Algebraic solution

3. The _____ is a function in mathematics. The application of this function to a value x is written as ex. Equivalently, this can be written in the form e^x, where e is a mathematical constant, the base of the natural logarithm, which equals approximately 2.718281828, and is also known as Euler's number.

   a. A Mathematical Theory of Communication
   b. A chemical equation
   c. Area hyperbolic functions
   d. Exponential function

4. The mathematical concept of a _____ expresses the intuitive idea of deterministic dependence between two quantities, one of which is viewed as primary and the other as secondary. A _____ then is a way to associate a unique output for each input of a specified type, for example, a real number or an element of a given set.

   a. Function
   b. Coherent
   c. Grill
   d. Going up

Chapter 3. Exponential and Logarithmic Functions

5. A _____ is a function that does not satisfy a polynomial equation whose coefficients are themselves polynomials, in contrast to an algebraic function, which does satisfy such an equation. In other words a _____ is a function which 'transcends' algebra in the sense that it cannot be expressed in terms of a finite sequence of the algebraic operations of addition, multiplication, and root extraction.

Examples of _____s include the exponential function, the logarithm, and the trigonometric functions.

a. 1-center problem
b. 120-cell
c. 2-3 heap
d. Transcendental function

6. In mathematics and computer science, _____ (also base-16, hexa or base, of 16. It uses sixteen distinct symbols, most often the symbols 0-9 to represent values zero to nine, and A, B, C, D, E, F (or a through f) to represent values ten to fifteen.

Its primary use is as a human friendly representation of binary coded values, so it is often used in digital electronics and computer engineering.

a. Hexadecimal
b. Radix
c. Factoradic
d. Tetradecimal

7. _____ is the concept of adding accumulated interest back to the principal, so that interest is earned on interest from that moment on. The act of declaring interest to be principal is called compounding. A loan, for example, may have its interest compounded every month: in this case, a loan with $100 principal and 1% interest per month would have a balance of $101 at the end of the first month.

a. Net interest margin
b. Net interest margin securities
c. Retained interest
d. Compound interest

8. In probability theory, a probability distribution is called _____ if its cumulative distribution function is _____. That is equivalent to saying that for random variables X with the distribution in question, Pr[X = a] = 0 for all real numbers a. If the distribution of X is _____ then X is called a _____ random variable.

Chapter 3. Exponential and Logarithmic Functions

a. Continuous
b. Conull set
c. Continuous phase modulation
d. Concatenated codes

9. _____ is a fee, paid on borrowed capital. Assets lent include money, shares, consumer goods through hire purchase, major assets such as aircraft, and even entire factories in finance lease arrangements. The _____ is calculated upon the value of the assets in the same manner as upon money.
a. A Mathematical Theory of Communication
b. Interest sensitivity gap
c. Interest
d. Interest expense

10. In mathematics and in the sciences, a _____ (plural: _____e, formulæ or _____s) is a concise way of expressing information symbolically (as in a mathematical or chemical _____), or a general relationship between quantities. One of many famous _____e is Albert Einstein's E = mc^2 (see special relativity

In mathematics, a _____ is a key to solve an equation with variables. For example, the problem of determining the volume of a sphere is one that requires a significant amount of integral calculus to solve.

a. 120-cell
b. 1-center problem
c. 2-3 heap
d. Formula

11. The function $\log_b(x)$ depends on both b and x, but the term _____ (or logarithmic function) in standard usage refers to a function of the form $\log_b(x)$ in which the base b is fixed and so the only argument is x. Thus there is one _____ for each value of the base b (which must be positive and must differ from 1.) Viewed in this way, the base-b _____ is the inverse function of the exponential function b^x.
a. 1-center problem
b. 120-cell
c. 2-3 heap
d. Logarithm function

12. In mathematics, the _____ of a number to a given base is the power or exponent to which the base must be raised in order to produce the number.

For example, the _____ of 1000 to the base 10 is 3, because 3 is how many 10s one must multiply to get 1000: thus 10 × 10 × 10 = 1000; the base-2 _____ of 32 is 5 because 5 is how many 2s one must multiply to get 32: thus 2 × 2 × 2 × 2 × 2 = 32. In the language of exponents: 10^3 = 1000, so $\log_{10} 1000 = 3$, and $2^5 = 32$, so $\log_2 32 = 5$.

a. 2-3 heap
b. Logarithm
c. 1-center problem
d. 120-cell

13. The _____, formerly known as the hyperbolic logarithm, is the logarithm to the base e, where e is an irrational constant approximately equal to 2.718 281 828. It is also sometimes referred to as the Napierian logarithm, although the original meaning of this term is slightly different. In simple terms, the _____ of a number x is the power to which e would have to be raised to equal x -- for example the natural log of e itself is 1 because $e^1 = e$, while the _____ of 1 would be 0, since $e^0 = 1$.

a. Logarithmic growth
b. Natural logarithm
c. 1-center problem
d. Logarithmic identities

14. In mathematics, _____ is the problem of finding what values fulfill a condition stated as an equality. Usually, this condition involves expressions with variables, which are to be substituted by values in order for the equality to hold. More precisely, an equation involves some free variables.

a. A posteriori
b. A Mathematical Theory of Communication
c. Equation solving
d. A chemical equation

15. A quantity is said to be subject to _____ if it decreases at a rate proportional to its value. Symbolically, this can be expressed as the following differential equation, where N is the quantity and λ is a positive number called the decay constant.

$$\frac{dN}{dt} = -\lambda N.$$

The solution to this equation is:

$$N(t) = N_0 e^{-\lambda t}.$$

Here is the quantity at time t, and $N_0 = N$ is the quantity, at time t = 0.

    a. Exponential formula
    b. Exponential decay
    c. Exponentiating by squaring
    d. Exponential integral

16. _____ occurs when the growth rate of a mathematical function is proportional to the function's current value. In the case of a discrete domain of definition with equal intervals it is also called geometric growth or geometric decay.

With _____ of a positive value its rate of increase steadily increases, or in the case of exponential decay, its rate of decrease steadily decreases.

    a. A posteriori
    b. A Mathematical Theory of Communication
    c. A chemical equation
    d. Exponential growth

17. A logistic function or _____ is the most common sigmoid curve. It models the S-curve of growth of some set P, where P might be thought of as population. The initial stage of growth is approximately exponential; then, as saturation begins, the growth slows, and at maturity, growth stops.
    a. Logarithmic integral function
    b. Lambert W function
    c. Logistic curve
    d. Polylogarithm

18. In mathematics, the concept of a _____ tries to capture the intuitive idea of a geometrical one-dimensional and continuous object. A simple example is the circle. In everyday use of the term '_____', a straight line is not curved, but in mathematical parlance _____s include straight lines and line segments.

a. Curve
b. Quadrifolium
c. Negative pedal curve
d. Kappa curve

Chapter 4. Trigonometry

1. In geometry and trigonometry, an _____ is the figure formed by two rays sharing a common endpoint, called the vertex of the _____. The magnitude of the _____ is the 'amount of rotation' that separates the two rays, and can be measured by considering the length of circular arc swept out when one ray is rotated about the vertex to coincide with the other. Where there is no possibility of confusion, the term '_____' is used interchangeably for both the geometric configuration itself and for its angular magnitude.
    a. A posteriori
    b. A Mathematical Theory of Communication
    c. A chemical equation
    d. Angle

2. Initial objects are also called _____, and terminal objects are also called final.
    a. Direct limit
    b. Coterminal
    c. Colimit
    d. Terminal object

3. A convention universally adopted in mathematical writing is that angles given a sign are _____ if measured anticlockwise, and negative angles if measured clockwise, from a given line. If no line is specified, it can be assumed to be the x-axis in the Cartesian plane. In many geometrical situations a negative angle of −θ is effectively equivalent to a positive angle of 'one full rotation less θ'.
    a. 2-3 heap
    b. 120-cell
    c. 1-center problem
    d. Positive angles

4. In algebraic geometry, _____ is a notion of genericity for a set of points, or other geometric objects. It means the general case situation, as opposed to some more special or coincidental cases that are possible. Its precise meaning differs in different settings.
    a. Lipschitz domain
    b. Compactness measure of a shape
    c. Convexity
    d. General position

5. _____ is a branch of mathematics that deals with triangles, particularly those plane triangles in which one angle has 90 degrees. _____ deals with relationships between the sides and the angles of triangles and with the trigonometric functions, which describe those relationships.

    _____ has applications in both pure mathematics and in applied mathematics, where it is essential in many branches of science and technology.

Chapter 4. Trigonometry

a. Trigonometric functions
b. Law of sines
c. Sine
d. Trigonometry

6. In geometry, a _____ is a special kind of point, usually a corner of a polygon, polyhedron, or higher dimensional polytope. In the geometry of curves a _____ is a point of where the first derivative of curvature is zero. In graph theory, a _____ is the fundamental unit out of which graphs are formed
a. Dini
b. Crib
c. Duality
d. Vertex

7. An angle smaller than a right angle is called an _____ (less than 90 degrees).
a. Integral geometry
b. Euclidean geometry
c. Ultraparallel theorem
d. Acute angle

8. A _____ is an angle whose Line is the center of a circle, and whose sides pass through a pair of points on the circle, thereby subtending an arc between those two points whose angle is equal to the _____ itself. It is also known as the arc segment's angular distance.

On a sphere or ellipsoid, the _____ is delineated along a great circle.

a. Line segment
b. Hypotenuse
c. Mirror image
d. Central angle

9. A _____ is a simple shape of Euclidean geometry consisting of those points in a plane which are at a constant distance, called the radius, from a fixed point, called the center. A _____ with center A is sometimes denoted by the symbol A.

A chord of a _____ is a line segment whose two endpoints lie on the _____.

a. Malfatti circles
b. Circumcircle
c. Circular segment
d. Circle

10. In mathematics the concept of a _____ generalizes notions such as 'length', 'area', and 'volume'. Informally, given some base set, a '_____' is any consistent assignment of 'sizes' to the subsets of the base set. Depending on the application, the 'size' of a subset may be interpreted as its physical size, the amount of something that lies within the subset, or the probability that some random process will yield a result within the subset.
   a. Measure
   b. Cusp
   c. Congruent
   d. Lattice

11. The _____ is a unit of plane angle, equal to 180/π degrees, or about 57.2958 degrees. It is the standard unit of angular measurement in all areas of mathematics beyond the elementary level.

The _____ is represented by the symbol 'rad' or, more rarely, by the superscript c.

   a. 1-center problem
   b. 2-3 heap
   c. 120-cell
   d. Radian

12. A pair of angles are complementary if the sum of their measures add up to 90 degrees.

If the two _____ are adjacent (i.e. have a common vertex and share a side, but do not have any interior points in common) their non-shared sides form a right angle.

In Euclidean geometry, the two acute angles in a right triangle are complementary, because there are 180>° in a triangle and 90>° have been accounted for by the right angle.

   a. Quincunx
   b. Conway polyhedron notation
   c. Complementary angles
   d. Hypotenuse

Chapter 4. Trigonometry

13. A pair of angles is _____ if their measurements add up to 180 degrees. If the two _____ angles are adjacent their non-shared sides form a straight line. The supplement of 135 would be 45.
   a. FISH
   b. Cylinder
   c. Dense
   d. Supplementary

14. Determining _____ was historically difficult. Although many methods were used for specific curves, the advent of calculus led to a general formula that provides closed-form solutions in some cases.

   A curve in, say, the plane can be approximated by connecting a finite number of points on the curve using line segments to create a polygonal path.

   a. Integral
   b. Indefinite integral
   c. Antidifferentiation
   d. Arc length

15. In mathematics, a _____ is a circle with a unit radius. Frequently, especially in trigonometry, 'the' _____ is the circle of radius 1 centered at the origin in the Cartesian coordinate system in the Euclidean plane. The _____ is often denoted S^1; the generalization to higher dimensions is the unit sphere.
   a. Excircle
   b. Inscribed angle theorem
   c. Open unit disk
   d. Unit circle

16. The mathematical concept of a _____ expresses the intuitive idea of deterministic dependence between two quantities, one of which is viewed as primary and the other as secondary. A _____ then is a way to associate a unique output for each input of a specified type, for example, a real number or an element of a given set.
   a. Function
   b. Going up
   c. Coherent
   d. Grill

17. _____ is a term in mathematics. It can refer to:

- a _____ line, in geometry
- the trigonometric function called _____
- the _____ method, a root-finding algorithm in numerical analysis

a. Large set
b. Secant
c. Separable
d. Solvable

18. The _____ of an angle is the ratio of the length of the opposite side to the length of the hypotenuse. In our case

$$\sin A = \frac{\text{opposite}}{\text{hypotenuse}} = \frac{a}{h}.$$

Note that this ratio does not depend on size of the particular right triangle chosen, as long as it contains the angle A, since all such triangles are similar.

The cosine of an angle is the ratio of the length of the adjacent side to the length of the hypotenuse.

a. Right angle
b. Law of sines
c. Trigonometric functions
d. Sine

19. In trigonometry, the _____ is a function defined as $\tan x = \sin x / \cos x$. The function is so-named because it can be defined as the length of a certain segment of a _____ (in the geometric sense) to the unit circle. In plane geometry, a line is _____ to a curve, at some point, if both line and curve pass through the point with the same direction.

a. Hopf conjectures
b. Projective connection
c. Conformal geometry
d. Tangent

20. In mathematics, the _____ functions are functions of an angle; they are important when studying triangles and modeling periodic phenomena, among many other applications.

Chapter 4. Trigonometry

a. Coversine
b. Law of sines
c. Gudermannian function
d. Trigonometric

21. In mathematics, the _____ are functions of an angle. They are important in the study of triangles and modeling periodic phenomena, among many other applications. _____ are commonly defined as ratios of two sides of a right triangle containing the angle, and can equivalently be defined as the lengths of various line segments from a unit circle.

   a. Trigonometric functions
   b. Sine
   c. Law of sines
   d. Trigonometric integrals

22. In mathematics, computing, linguistics and related subjects, an _____ is a sequence of finite instructions, often used for calculation and data processing. It is formally a type of effective method in which a list of well-defined instructions for completing a task will, when given an initial state, proceed through a well-defined series of successive states, eventually terminating in an end-state. The transition from one state to the next is not necessarily deterministic; some _____s, known as probabilistic _____s, incorporate randomness.

   a. Algorithm
   b. Out-of-core
   c. Approximate counting algorithm
   d. In-place algorithm

23. In mathematics, a _____ is a number that can be expressed as an integral of an algebraic function over an algebraic domain. Kontsevich and Zagier define a _____ as a complex number whose real and imaginary parts are values of absolutely convergent integrals of rational functions with rational coefficients, over domains in given by polynomial inequalities with rational coefficients.

   a. Period
   b. Disk
   c. Boussinesq approximation
   d. Closeness

24. In mathematics, a _____ is a function that repeats its values after some definite period has been added to its independent variable. This property is called periodicity. An illustration of a _____ with period P.

Everyday examples are seen when the variable is time; for instance the hands of a clock or the phases of the moon show periodic behaviour.

a. Calculus controversy
b. Method of indivisibles
c. Hyperbolic angle
d. Periodic function

25. In mathematics, especially in the area of abstract algebra known as ring theory, a _____ is a ring with 0 ≠ 1 such that ab = 0 implies that either a = 0 or b = 0. That is, it is a nontrivial ring without left or right zero divisors. A commutative _____ is called an integral _____.

a. Domain
b. Modular representation theory
c. Left primitive ring
d. Simple ring

26. In descriptive statistics, the _____ is the length of the smallest interval which contains all the data. It is calculated by subtracting the smallest observations from the greatest and provides an indication of statistical dispersion.

It is measured in the same units as the data.

a. Bandwidth
b. Range
c. Kernel
d. Class

27. _____ is an adjective meaning contiguous, adjoining or abutting.

In geometry, _____ is when sides meet to make an angle.

In trigonometry the _____ side of a right angled triangle is the cathetus next to the angle in question.

a. Ambient space
b. Ordered geometry
c. Affine geometry
d. Adjacent

28. A _____ is the longest side of a right triangle, the side opposite of the right angle. The length of the _____ of a right triangle can be found using the Pythagorean theorem, which states that the square of the length of the _____ equals the sum of the squares of the lengths of the two other sides.

Chapter 4. Trigonometry

For example, if one of the other sides has a length of 3 meters and the other has a length of 4 m.

   a. Hypotenuse
   b. Concyclic points
   c. Golden angle
   d. Reflection symmetry

29. In mathematics, the _____ of a number n is the number that, when added to n, yields zero. The _____ of n is denoted −n. For example, 7 is −7, because 7 + (−7) = 0, and the _____ of −0.3 is 0.3, because −0.3 + 0.3 = 0.

   a. Additive inverse
   b. Algebraic structure
   c. Associativity
   d. Arity

30. A _____ is one of the basic shapes of geometry: a polygon with three corners or vertices and three sides or edges which are line segments. A _____ with vertices A, B, and C is denoted ABC.

In Euclidean geometry any three non-collinear points determine a unique _____ and a unique plane.

   a. Fuhrmann circle
   b. Kepler triangle
   c. 1-center problem
   d. Triangle

31. In mathematics, the concept of a _____ tries to capture the intuitive idea of a geometrical one-dimensional and continuous object. A simple example is the circle. In everyday use of the term '_____', a straight line is not curved, but in mathematical parlance _____s include straight lines and line segments.

   a. Quadrifolium
   b. Negative pedal curve
   c. Kappa curve
   d. Curve

32. In mathematics, a _____ is the end result of a division problem. It can also be expressed as the number of times the divisor divides into the dividend.

Chapter 4. Trigonometry

   a. Limiting
   b. Marginal cost
   c. Notation
   d. Quotient

33. In mathematics, the multiplicative inverse of a number x, denoted 1/x or x $^{-1}$, is the number which, when multiplied by x, yields 1. The multiplicative inverse of x is also called the _____ of x.
   a. 2-3 heap
   b. 1-center problem
   c. 120-cell
   d. Reciprocal

34. In mathematics, _____ are equalities that involve trigonometric functions that are true for every single value of the occurring variables. These identities are useful whenever expressions involving trigonometric functions need to be simplified. An important application is the integration of non-trigonometric functions: a common trick involves first using the substitution rule with a trigonometric function, and then simplifying the resulting integral with a trigonometric identity.
   a. 120-cell
   b. Trigonometric identities
   c. 2-3 heap
   d. 1-center problem

35. The Q-TIP of a geographic location is its height above a fixed reference point, often the mean sea level. _____, or geometric height, is mainly used when referring to points on the Earth's surface, while altitude or geopotential height is used for points above the surface, such as an aircraft in flight or a spacecraft in orbit.

Less commonly, _____ is measured using the center of the Earth as the reference point.

   a. A Mathematical Theory of Communication
   b. A posteriori
   c. A chemical equation
   d. Elevation

36. In abstract algebra, a field extension L /K is called _____ if every element of L is _____ over K. Field extensions which are not _____.

For example, the field extension R/Q, that is the field of real numbers as an extension of the field of rational numbers, is transcendental, while the field extensions C/R and Q

a. Echo
b. Algebraic
c. Ideal
d. Identity

37. _____ is the magnitude of change in the oscillating variable, with each oscillation, within an oscillating system. For instance, sound waves are oscillations in atmospheric pressure and their _____s are proportional to the change in pressure during one oscillation. If the variable undergoes regular oscillations, and a graph of the system is drawn with the oscillating variable as the vertical axis and time as the horizontal axis, the _____ is visually represented by the vertical distance between the extrema of the curve.
   a. Areal velocity
   b. Angular velocity
   c. Angular frequency
   d. Amplitude

38.

_____ is a technique used in electronic communication, most commonly for transmitting information via a radio carrier wave. AM works by varying the strength of the transmitted signal in relation to the information being sent. For example, changes in the signal strength can be used to reflect the sounds to be reproduced by a speaker, or to specify the light intensity of television pixels.

   a. A chemical equation
   b. A posteriori
   c. A Mathematical Theory of Communication
   d. Amplitude modulation

39. In telecommunications, _____ is the process of varying a periodic waveform. Normally a high-frequency sinusoid waveform is used as carrier signal. The three key parameters of a sine wave are its amplitude, its phase and its frequency, all of which can be modified in accordance with a low frequency information signal to obtain the modulated signal.
   a. 120-cell
   b. 1-center problem
   c. 2-3 heap
   d. Modulation

40. _____ is any effect, either deliberately engendered or inherent to a system, that tends to reduce the amplitude of oscillations of an oscillatory system.

In physics and engineering, _____ may be mathematically modelled as a force synchronous with the velocity of the object but opposite in direction to it. If such force is also proportional to the velocity, as for a simple mechanical viscous damper, the force F may be related to the velocity v by

$$\mathbf{F} = -c\mathbf{v}$$

where c is the viscous _____ coefficient, given in units of newton-seconds per meter.

a. Damping
b. 120-cell
c. 1-center problem
d. Vibrating string

41. In mathematics, the _____ is a test used to determine if a function is injective, surjective or bijective.

Suppose there is a function f : X → Y with a graph., and you have a horizontal line of X x Y :
$$y_0 \in Y, \{(x, y_0) : x \in X\} = (X \times y_0)$$

- If the function is injective, then it can be visualized as one whose graph is never intersected by any horizontal line more than once.
- Iff f is surjective any horizontal line will intersect the graph at least at one point
- If f is bijective any horizontal line will intersect the graph at exactly one point.

This test is also used to find whether or not the inverse of the function is indeed a function as well. This is due to the reflective properties of the function over y=x.

a. Disjoint sets
b. Subset
c. Multiset
d. Horizontal Line Test

42. An _____ is a function which does the reverse of a given function.
a. Empty set
b. Empty function
c. A Mathematical Theory of Communication
d. Inverse function

Chapter 4. Trigonometry

43. In mathematics, the _____ or cyclometric functions are the so-called inverse functions of the trigonometric functions, though they do not meet the official definition for inverse functions as their domains are subsets of the images of the original functions.
    a. A Mathematical Theory of Communication
    b. A posteriori
    c. A chemical equation
    d. Inverse trigonometric functions

44. In acoustics and telecommunication, the _____ of a wave is a component frequency of the signal that is an integer multiple of the fundamental frequency. For example, if the frequency is f, the _____s have frequency 2f, 3f, 4f, etc, as well as f itself. The _____s have the property that they are all periodic at the signal frequency.
    a. Digital room correction
    b. Subharmonic
    c. Robinson-Dadson curves
    d. Harmonic

45. In abstract algebra, a module S over a ring R is called _____ or irreducible if it is not the zero module 0 and if its only submodules are 0 and S. Understanding the _____ modules over a ring is usually helpful because these modules form the 'building blocks' of all other modules in a certain sense.

    Abelian groups are the same as Z-modules.

    a. Derivation
    b. Basis
    c. Harmonic series
    d. Simple

46. _____ is the motion of a simple harmonic oscillator, a motion that is neither driven nor damped. The motion is periodic, as it repeats itself at standard intervals in a specific manner - described as being sinusoidal, with constant amplitude. It is characterized by its amplitude, its period which is the time for a single oscillation, its frequency which is the number of cycles per unit time, and its phase, which determines the starting point on the sine wave.
    a. Stretch rule
    b. Kinematics
    c. Configuration space
    d. Simple harmonic motion

47. In mathematics, the _____ or Pythagoras' theorem is a relation in Euclidean geometry among the three sides of a right triangle. The theorem is named after the Greek mathematician Pythagoras, who by tradition is credited with its discovery and proof, although it is often argued that knowledge of the theory predates him.. The theorem is as follows:

In any right triangle, the area of the square whose side is the hypotenuse is equal to the sum of the areas of the squares whose sides are the two legs.

   a. 120-cell
   b. Pythagorean Theorem
   c. 2-3 heap
   d. 1-center problem

48. In mathematics, a _____ is a statement that can be proved on the basis of explicitly stated or previously agreed assumptions.
   a. Disjunction introduction
   b. Logical value
   c. Boolean function
   d. Theorem

Chapter 5. Analytic Trigonometry

1. In mathematics, a function f is _____ of a function g if f whenever A and B are complementary angles. This definition typically applies to trigonometric functions.
    a. Birkhoff interpolation
    b. Balian-Low theorem
    c. Boxcar function
    d. Cofunction

2. In mathematics, a _____ is the end result of a division problem. It can also be expressed as the number of times the divisor divides into the dividend.
    a. Notation
    b. Marginal cost
    c. Quotient
    d. Limiting

3. In mathematics, the multiplicative inverse of a number x, denoted 1/x or x^{-1}, is the number which, when multiplied by x, yields 1. The multiplicative inverse of x is also called the _____ of x.
    a. Reciprocal
    b. 2-3 heap
    c. 1-center problem
    d. 120-cell

4. In mathematics, the _____ functions are functions of an angle; they are important when studying triangles and modeling periodic phenomena, among many other applications.
    a. Trigonometric
    b. Gudermannian function
    c. Law of sines
    d. Coversine

5. In mathematics, _____ are equalities that involve trigonometric functions that are true for every single value of the occurring variables. These identities are useful whenever expressions involving trigonometric functions need to be simplified. An important application is the integration of non-trigonometric functions: a common trick involves first using the substitution rule with a trigonometric function, and then simplifying the resulting integral with a trigonometric identity.
    a. 1-center problem
    b. Trigonometric identities
    c. 2-3 heap
    d. 120-cell

Chapter 5. Analytic Trigonometry

6. The mathematical concept of a _____ expresses the intuitive idea of deterministic dependence between two quantities, one of which is viewed as primary and the other as secondary. A _____ then is a way to associate a unique output for each input of a specified type, for example, a real number or an element of a given set.
   a. Grill
   b. Going up
   c. Coherent
   d. Function

7. In mathematics, a _____ is any function which can be written as the ratio of two polynomial functions. _____ of degree 2 :

$$y = \frac{x^2 - 3x - 2}{x^2 - 4}$$

In the case of one variable, x, a _____ is a function of the form

$$f(x) = \frac{P(x)}{Q(x)}$$

where P and Q are polynomial function in x and Q is not the zero polynomial. The domain of f is the set of all points x for which the denominator Q

   a. Rational function
   b. 120-cell
   c. 1-center problem
   d. Legendre rational functions

8. _____ is a quantity expressing the two-dimensional size of a defined part of a surface, typically a region bounded by a closed curve. The term surface _____ refers to the total _____ of the exposed surface of a 3-dimensional solid, such as the sum of the _____ s of the exposed sides of a polyhedron. _____ is an important invariant in the differential geometry of surfaces.
   a. A chemical equation
   b. A Mathematical Theory of Communication
   c. Area
   d. A posteriori

9. In mathematics and in the sciences, a _____ (plural: _____ e, formulæ or _____ s) is a concise way of expressing information symbolically (as in a mathematical or chemical _____), or a general relationship between quantities. One of many famous _____ e is Albert Einstein's E = mc² (see special relativity

In mathematics, a _____ is a key to solve an equation with variables. For example, the problem of determining the volume of a sphere is one that requires a significant amount of integral calculus to solve.

a. 120-cell
b. 2-3 heap
c. 1-center problem
d. Formula

10. In mathematics, the _____ are functions of an angle. They are important in the study of triangles and modeling periodic phenomena, among many other applications. _____ are commonly defined as ratios of two sides of a right triangle containing the angle, and can equivalently be defined as the lengths of various line segments from a unit circle.
a. Trigonometric functions
b. Trigonometric integrals
c. Sine
d. Law of sines

11. In geometry and trigonometry, an _____ is the figure formed by two rays sharing a common endpoint, called the vertex of the _____. The magnitude of the _____ is the 'amount of rotation' that separates the two rays, and can be measured by considering the length of circular arc swept out when one ray is rotated about the vertex to coincide with the other. Where there is no possibility of confusion, the term '_____' is used interchangeably for both the geometric configuration itself and for its angular magnitude.
a. Angle
b. A posteriori
c. A Mathematical Theory of Communication
d. A chemical equation

12. _____ is the concept of adding accumulated interest back to the principal, so that interest is earned on interest from that moment on. The act of declaring interest to be principal is called compounding. A loan, for example, may have its interest compounded every month: in this case, a loan with $100 principal and 1% interest per month would have a balance of $101 at the end of the first month.
a. Net interest margin
b. Retained interest
c. Net interest margin securities
d. Compound interest

13. In probability theory, a probability distribution is called _____ if its cumulative distribution function is _____. That is equivalent to saying that for random variables X with the distribution in question, Pr[X = a] = 0 for all real numbers a. If the distribution of X is _____ then X is called a _____ random variable.
   a. Concatenated codes
   b. Continuous phase modulation
   c. Continuous
   d. Conull set

14. _____ is a fee, paid on borrowed capital. Assets lent include money, shares, consumer goods through hire purchase, major assets such as aircraft, and even entire factories in finance lease arrangements. The _____ is calculated upon the value of the assets in the same manner as upon money.
   a. Interest
   b. A Mathematical Theory of Communication
   c. Interest expense
   d. Interest sensitivity gap

Chapter 6. Additional Topics in Trigonometry

1. The _____, in trigonometry, is a statement about any triangle in a plane. Where the sides of the triangle are a, b and c and the angles opposite those sides are A, B and C, then the _____ states equality of the first three quantities below:

$$\underbrace{\frac{a}{\sin A} = \frac{b}{\sin B} = \frac{c}{\sin C}}_{\text{Law of sines}} = 2R$$

where R is the radius of the triangle's circumcircle. The _____ is also sometimes stated as

$$\frac{\sin A}{a} = \frac{\sin B}{b} = \frac{\sin C}{c}.$$

This law is useful when computing the remaining sides of a triangle if two angles and a side are known, a common problem in the technique of triangulation.

   a. Trigonometric functions
   b. Trigonometric
   c. Sine integral
   d. Law of Sines

2. The _____ of an angle is the ratio of the length of the opposite side to the length of the hypotenuse. In our case

$$\sin A = \frac{\text{opposite}}{\text{hypotenuse}} = \frac{a}{h}.$$

Note that this ratio does not depend on size of the particular right triangle chosen, as long as it contains the angle A, since all such triangles are similar.

The cosine of an angle is the ratio of the length of the adjacent side to the length of the hypotenuse.

   a. Trigonometric functions
   b. Sine
   c. Right angle
   d. Law of sines

3. A _____ is one of the basic shapes of geometry: a polygon with three corners or vertices and three sides or edges which are line segments. A _____ with vertices A, B, and C is denoted ABC.

In Euclidean geometry any three non-collinear points determine a unique _____ and a unique plane.

a. Triangle
b. Kepler triangle
c. 1-center problem
d. Fuhrmann circle

4. _____ is a quantity expressing the two-dimensional size of a defined part of a surface, typically a region bounded by a closed curve. The term surface _____ refers to the total _____ of the exposed surface of a 3-dimensional solid, such as the sum of the _____s of the exposed sides of a polyhedron. _____ is an important invariant in the differential geometry of surfaces.
   a. A Mathematical Theory of Communication
   b. Area
   c. A chemical equation
   d. A posteriori

5. In trigonometry, the _____ is a statement about a general triangle which relates the lengths of its sides to the cosine of one of its angles. Using notation as in Fig. 1, the _____ states that

$$c^2 = a^2 + b^2 - 2ab\cos(\gamma),$$

or, equivalently:

$$b^2 = c^2 + a^2 - 2ca\cos(\beta),$$
$$a^2 = b^2 + c^2 - 2bc\cos(\alpha),$$
$$\cos(\gamma) = \frac{a^2 + b^2 - c^2}{2ab}.$$

Note that c is the side opposite of angle γ, and that a and b are the two sides enclosing γ.

   a. Law of Cosines
   b. Trigonometric
   c. Trigonometric functions
   d. Law of tangents

6. _____, also sometimes known as standard form or as exponential notation, is a way of writing numbers that accommodates values too large or small to be conveniently written in standard decimal notation. _____ has a number of useful properties and is often favored by scientists, mathematicians and engineers, who work with such numbers.

Chapter 6. Additional Topics in Trigonometry　　　　　　　　　　　　　　　　　　　　　61

In _____, numbers are written in the form:

$$a \times 10^b$$

   a. Radix point
   b. Leading zero
   c. 1-center problem
   d. Scientific notation

7. In mathematics, the _____s are an extension of the real numbers obtained by adjoining an imaginary unit, denoted i, which satisfies:

$$i^2 = -1.$$

Every _____ can be written in the form a + bi, where a and b are real numbers called the real part and the imaginary part of the _____, respectively.

_____s are a field, and thus have addition, subtraction, multiplication, and division operations. These operations extend the corresponding operations on real numbers, although with a number of additional elegant and useful properties, e.g., negative real numbers can be obtained by squaring _____s.

   a. Real part
   b. 120-cell
   c. 1-center problem
   d. Complex number

8. In mathematics and in the sciences, a _____ (plural: _____e, formulæ or _____s) is a concise way of expressing information symbolically (as in a mathematical or chemical _____), or a general relationship between quantities. One of many famous _____e is Albert Einstein's E = mc² (see special relativity

In mathematics, a _____ is a key to solve an equation with variables. For example, the problem of determining the volume of a sphere is one that requires a significant amount of integral calculus to solve.

   a. 120-cell
   b. 2-3 heap
   c. 1-center problem
   d. Formula

9. Initial objects are also called _____, and terminal objects are also called final.
   a. Colimit
   b. Coterminal
   c. Terminal object
   d. Direct limit

10. In trigonometry, the _____ is a function defined as $\tan x = \sin x / \cos x$. The function is so-named because it can be defined as the length of a certain segment of a _____ (in the geometric sense) to the unit circle. In plane geometry, a line is _____ to a curve, at some point, if both line and curve pass through the point with the same direction.
    a. Conformal geometry
    b. Projective connection
    c. Hopf conjectures
    d. Tangent

11. In geometry, the _____ to a curve at a given point is the straight line that 'just touches' the curve at that point. As it passes through the point of tangency, the _____ is 'going in the same direction' as the curve, and in this sense it is the best straight-line approximation to the curve at that point. The same definition applies to space curves and curves in n-dimensional Euclidean space.
    a. Darboux frame
    b. Four-vertex theorem
    c. Chern-Weil theory
    d. Tangent line

12. In physics and in _____ calculus, a _____ is a concept characterized by a magnitude and a direction. A _____ can be thought of as an arrow in Euclidean space, drawn from an initial point A pointing to a terminal point B.
    a. Dominance
    b. Deviation
    c. Constraint
    d. Vector

13. In geometry, a _____ is a part of a line that is bounded by two distinct end points, and contains every point on the line between its end points. Examples of _____s include the sides of a triangle or square. More generally, when the end points are both vertices of a polygon, the _____ is either an edge if they are adjacent vertices, or otherwise a diagonal.

a. Cuboid
b. Line segment
c. Transversal line
d. Golden angle

14. In mathematics, the _____ is a conic section, the intersection of a right circular conical surface and a plane parallel to a generating straight line of that surface. Given a point and a line that lie in a plane, the locus of points in that plane that are equidistant to them is a _____.

A particular case arises when the plane is tangent to the conical surface of a circle.

a. Directrix
b. Matrix representation of conic sections
c. Dandelin sphere
d. Parabola

15. In mathematics, a _____ is, informally, an infinitely vast and infinitely thin sheet. _____s may be thought of as objects in some higher dimensional space, or they may be considered without any outside space, as in the setting of Euclidean geometry
a. Blocking
b. Bandwidth
c. Group
d. Plane

16. In algebraic geometry, _____ is a notion of genericity for a set of points, or other geometric objects. It means the general case situation, as opposed to some more special or coincidental cases that are possible. Its precise meaning differs in different settings.
a. Compactness measure of a shape
b. Convexity
c. Lipschitz domain
d. General position

17. The mathematical concept of a _____ expresses the intuitive idea of deterministic dependence between two quantities, one of which is viewed as primary and the other as secondary. A _____ then is a way to associate a unique output for each input of a specified type, for example, a real number or an element of a given set.

a. Function
b. Grill
c. Going up
d. Coherent

18. In mathematics, _____ is one of the basic operations defining a vector space in linear algebra. Note that _____ is different from scalar product which is an inner product between two vectors.

More specifically, if K is a field and V is a vector space over K, then _____ is a function from K × V to V.

a. Jordan normal form
b. Scalar multiplication
c. Non-negative matrix factorization
d. Frobenius normal form

19. In geometry, a _____ is a quadrilateral with two sets of parallel sides. The opposite sides of a _____ are of equal length, and the opposite angles of a _____ are congruent. The three-dimensional counterpart of a _____ is a parallelepiped.

a. 1-center problem
b. 2-3 heap
c. Parallelogram
d. 120-cell

20. In mathematics, the simplest form of the _____ belongs to elementary geometry. It states that the sum of the squares of the lengths of the four sides of a parallelogram equals the sum of the squares of the lengths of the two diagonals. With the notation in the diagram on the right, this can be stated as

$$(AB)^2 + (BC)^2 + (CD)^2 + (DA)^2 = (AC)^2 + (BD)^2.$$

In case the parallelogram is a rectangle, the two diagonals are of equal lengths and the statement reduces to the Pythagorean theorem.

a. Homothetic center
b. Half-space
c. Square lattice
d. Parallelogram law

Chapter 6. Additional Topics in Trigonometry

21. _____ is the mathematical operation of scaling one number by another. It is one of the four basic operations in elementary arithmetic.

_____ is defined for whole numbers in terms of repeated addition; for example, 4 multiplied by 3 can be calculated by adding 3 copies of 4 together:

$$4 + 4 + 4 = 12.$$

_____ of rational numbers and real numbers is defined by systematic generalization of this basic idea.

a. Least common multiple
b. Multiplication
c. The number 0 is even.
d. Highest common factor

22. In mathematics, _____ are a concept central to linear algebra and related fields of mathematics

Suppose that K is a field and V is a vector space over K.

a. Linear combinations
b. Linear span
c. Setoid
d. Polarization

23. In combinatorial mathematics, a _____ is an un-ordered collection of distinct elements, usually of a prescribed size and taken from a given set. Given such a set S, a _____ of elements of S is just a subset of S, where as always forsets the order of the elements is not taken into account. Also, as always forsets, no elements can be repeated more than once in a _____; this is often referred to as a 'collection without repetition'.

a. Combination
b. Fill-in
c. Heawood number
d. Sparsity

24. In geometry and trigonometry, an _____ is the figure formed by two rays sharing a common endpoint, called the vertex of the _____. The magnitude of the _____ is the 'amount of rotation' that separates the two rays, and can be measured by considering the length of circular arc swept out when one ray is rotated about the vertex to coincide with the other. Where there is no possibility of confusion, the term '_____' is used interchangeably for both the geometric configuration itself and for its angular magnitude.

a. A Mathematical Theory of Communication
b. A posteriori
c. A chemical equation
d. Angle

25. In mathematics, the _____ is an operation which takes two vectors over the real numbers R and returns a real-valued scalar quantity. It is the standard inner product of the orthonormal Euclidean space.

The _____ of two vectors a = [a_1, a_2, …, a_n] and b = [b_1, b_2, …, b_n] is defined as:

$$\mathbf{a} \cdot \mathbf{b} = \sum_{i=1}^{n} a_i b_i = a_1 b_1 + a_2 b_2 + \cdots + a_n b_n$$

where Σ denotes summation notation and n is the dimension of the vectors.

a. Matrix determinant lemma
b. Dot product
c. Principal axis theorem
d. Conjugate transpose

26. In mathematics, two vectors are _____ if they are perpendicular. For example, a subway and the street above, although they do not physically intersect, are _____ if they cross at a right angle.
a. Unique factorization domain
b. Algebraic structure
c. Additive identity
d. Orthogonal

27. In linear algebra and functional analysis, a _____ is a linear transformation P from a vector space to itself such that P^2 = P. It leaves its image unchanged. Though abstract, this definition of '_____' formalizes and generalizes the idea of graphical _____.
a. Characteristic function
b. Critical point
c. Deviance
d. Projection

Chapter 6. Additional Topics in Trigonometry

28. In mathematics, the _____ is a geometric representation of the complex numbers established by the real axis and the orthogonal imaginary axis. It can be thought of as a modified Cartesian plane, with the real part of a complex number represented by a displacement along the x-axis, and the imaginary part by a displacement along the y-axis.

The _____ is sometimes called the Argand plane because it is used in Argand diagrams.

   a. 2-3 heap
   b. 1-center problem
   c. 120-cell
   d. Complex plane

29. In mathematics, an _____ is a complex number whose squared value is a real number less than or equal to zero. The imaginary unit, denoted by i or j, is an example of an _____. If y is a real number, then iÂ·y is an _____, because:

$$(i \cdot y)^2 = i^2 \cdot y^2 = -y^2 \leq 0.$$

They were defined in 1572 by Rafael Bombelli.

   a. A chemical equation
   b. A posteriori
   c. Imaginary number
   d. A Mathematical Theory of Communication

30. In mathematics, the _____ of a real number is its numerical value without regard to its sign. So, for example, 3 is the _____ of both 3 and −3.

The _____ of a number a is denoted by $|a|$.

Generalizations of the _____ for real numbers occur in a wide variety of mathematical settings.

   a. Area hyperbolic functions
   b. A Mathematical Theory of Communication
   c. Absolute value
   d. A chemical equation

31. In mathematics, and in particular in abstract algebra, distributivity is a property of binary operations that generalises the _____ law from elementary algebra.

a. Permutation
b. Closure with a twist
c. General linear group
d. Distributive

32. In mathematics, the _____ functions are functions of an angle; they are important when studying triangles and modeling periodic phenomena, among many other applications.
    a. Trigonometric
    b. Gudermannian function
    c. Coversine
    d. Law of sines

33. In mathematics, a _____ is the end result of a division problem. It can also be expressed as the number of times the divisor divides into the dividend.
    a. Limiting
    b. Marginal cost
    c. Quotient
    d. Notation

34. In mathematics, a _____ is a statement that can be proved on the basis of explicitly stated or previously agreed assumptions.
    a. Disjunction introduction
    b. Logical value
    c. Boolean function
    d. Theorem

35. In vascular plants, the _____ is the organ of a plant body that typically lies below the surface of the soil. This is not always the case, however, since a _____ can also be aerial (that is, growing above the ground) or aerating (that is, growing up above the ground or especially above water.) Furthermore, a stem normally occurring below ground is not exceptional either
    a. 2-3 heap
    b. 1-center problem
    c. 120-cell
    d. Root

36. In mathematics, the nth _____ are all the complex numbers which yield 1 when raised to a given power n. It can be shown that they are located on the unit circle of the complex plane and that in that plane they form the vertices of an n-sided regular polygon with one vertex on 1.
   a. Square root of 2
   b. Roots of unity
   c. 120-cell
   d. 1-center problem

Chapter 7. Systems of Equations and Inequalities

1. In linear algebra, _____ is a version of Gaussian elimination that puts zeros both above and below each pivot element as it goes from the top row of the given matrix to the bottom. In other words, _____ brings a matrix to reduced row echelon form, whereas Gaussian elimination takes it only as far as row echelon form. Every matrix has a reduced row echelon form, and this algorithm is guaranteed to produce it.
   a. Conservation form
   b. Spheroidal wave functions
   c. Lax equivalence theorem
   d. Gauss-Jordan elimination

2. _____ is a form where m is the slope of the line and b is the y-intercept, which is the y-coordinate of the point where the line crosses the y axis. This can be seen by letting x = 0, which immediately gives y = b.
   a. Commutative law
   b. Dynamical system
   c. Separable extension
   d. Slope-intercept form

3. In mathematics, the _____ of two sets A and B is the set that contains all elements of A that also belong to B, but no other elements.

For explanation of the symbols used in this article, refer to the table of mathematical symbols.

The _____ of A and B

The _____ of A and B is written 'A ∩ B'. Formally:

> x is an element of A ∩ B if and only if
> - x is an element of A and
> - x is an element of B.
>
> For example:
> - The _____ of the sets {1, 2, 3} and {2, 3, 4} is {2, 3}.
> - The number 9 is not in the _____ of the set of prime numbers {2, 3, 5, 7, 11, …} and the set of odd numbers {1, 3, 5, 7, 9, 11, …}.

If the _____ of two sets A and B is empty, that is they have no elements in common, then they are said to be disjoint, denoted: A ∩ B = ∅. For example the sets {1, 2} and {3, 4} are disjoint, written {1, 2} ∩ {3, 4} = ∅.

Chapter 7. Systems of Equations and Inequalities

    a. Intersection
    b. Erlang
    c. Order
    d. Advice

4. In economics, specifically cost accounting, the _____ is the point at which cost or expenses and revenue are equal: there is no net loss or gain, and one has 'broken even'. Therefore has not made a profit or a loss.

In the linear Cost-Volume-Profit Analysis model, the _____ can be directly computed in terms of Total Revenue and Total Costs as:

$$TR = TC$$
$$P \times X = TFC + V \times X$$
$$P \times X - V \times X = TFC$$
$$(P - V) \times X = TFC$$
$$X = \frac{TFC}{P - V}$$

where:

- TFC is Total Fixed Costs,
- P is Unit Sale Price, and
- V is Unit Variable Cost.

The _____ can alternatively be computed as the point where Contribution equals Fixed Costs.

The quantity $(P - V)$ is of interest in its own right, and is called the Unit Contribution Margin: it is the marginal profit per unit, or alternatively the portion of each sale that contributes to Fixed Costs. Thus the _____ can be more simply computed as the point where Total Contribution = Total Fixed Cost:

$$\text{Total Contribution} = \text{Total Fixed Costs}$$
$$\text{Unit Contribution} \times \text{Number of Units} = \text{Total Fixed Costs}$$
$$\text{Number of Units} = \frac{\text{Total Fixed Costs}}{\text{Unit Contribution}}$$

In currency units to reach break-even, one can use the above calculation and multiply by Price, or equivalently use the Contribution Margin Ratio to compute it as:

$$\text{Break-even(in Sales)} = \frac{\text{Fixed Costs}}{C/P}.$$

R=C Where R is revenue generated C is cost incurred.

a. 1-center problem
b. Small numbers game
c. Break-even point
d. 120-cell

5. In the study of metric spaces in mathematics, there are various notions of two metrics on the same underlying space being 'the same', or _____.

In the following, M will denote a non-empty set and d_1 and d_2 will denote two metrics on M.

The two metrics d_1 and d_2 are said to be topologically _____ if they generate the same topology on M.

a. A chemical equation
b. A posteriori
c. A Mathematical Theory of Communication
d. Equivalent

6. In logic, a theory is _____ if it does not contain a contradiction. The lack of contradiction can be defined in either semantic or syntactic terms. The semantic definition states that a theory is _____ if it has a model; this is the sense used in traditional Aristotelian logic, although in contemporary mathematical logic the term satisfiable is used instead.

a. Consistent
b. Second-order logic
c. First-order logic
d. Logic

7. In mathematics, a _____ is a collection of linear equations involving the same set of variables. For example,

$$\begin{aligned} 3x + 2y - z &= 1 \\ 2x - 2y + 4z &= -2 \\ -x + \tfrac{1}{2}y - z &= 0 \end{aligned}$$

is a system of three equations in the three variables x, y, z. A solution to a linear system is an assignment of numbers to the variables such that all the equations are simultaneously satisfied.

Chapter 7. Systems of Equations and Inequalities

a. Hypsometric equation
b. System of linear equations
c. Quintic equation
d. Slutsky equation

8. A _____ is an algebraic equation in which each term is either a constant or the product of a constant and a single variable. _____s can have one, two, three or more variables.

_____s occur with great regularity in applied mathematics.

a. Quadratic equation
b. Difference of two squares
c. Quartic equation
d. Linear equation

9. In quantum field theory and statistical mechanics in the thermodynamic limit, a system with a global symmetry can have more than one phase. For parameters where the symmetry is spontaneously broken, the system is said to be _____. When the global symmetry is unbroken the system is disordered.
   a. Isoenthalpic-isobaric ensemble
   b. Ursell function
   c. Ordered
   d. Einstein relation

10. In linear algebra a matrix is in _____ if

    - All nonzero rows are above any rows of all zeroes, and
    - The leading coefficient of a row is always strictly to the right of the leading coefficient of the row above it.

This is the definition used in this article, but some texts add a third condition:

- The leading coefficient of each nonzero row is one.

A matrix is in reduced row echelon form if it satisfies the above three conditions, and if, in addition

- Every leading coefficient is the only nonzero entry in its column.

The first non-zero entry in each row is called a pivot.

This matrix is in reduced row echelon form:

$$\begin{bmatrix} 0 & 1 & 4 & 0 & 0 \\ 0 & 0 & 0 & 1 & 0 \\ 0 & 0 & 0 & 0 & 1 \\ 0 & 0 & 0 & 0 & 0 \end{bmatrix}.$$

The following matrix is also in row echelon form, but not in reduced row form:

$$\begin{bmatrix} 1 & 1 & 1 & 1 \\ 0 & 9 & 0 & 2 \\ 0 & 0 & 0 & 3 \end{bmatrix}.$$

However, this matrix is not in row echelon form, as the leading coefficient of row 3 is not strictly to the right of the leading coefficient of row 2.

$$\begin{bmatrix} 1 & 2 & 3 & 4 \\ 0 & 3 & 7 & 2 \\ 0 & 2 & 0 & 0 \end{bmatrix}$$

Every non-zero matrix can be reduced to an infinite number of echelon forms via elementary matrix transformations.

   a. Circulant matrix
   b. Folded spectrum method
   c. Power iteration
   d. Row-echelon form

11.   In linear algebra, _____ is an efficient algorithm for solving systems of linear equations, finding the rank of a matrix, and calculating the inverse of an invertible square matrix. _____ is named after German mathematician and scientist Carl Friedrich Gauss.

Elementary row operations are used to reduce a matrix to row echelon form.

a. Gaussian elimination
b. Conjugate gradient method
c. Crout matrix decomposition
d. Cholesky decomposition

12. A _____ is a mathematical model of a system based on the use of a linear operator. _____s typically exhibit features and properties that are much simpler than the general, nonlinear case. As a mathematical abstraction or idealization, _____s find important applications in automatic control theory, signal processing, and telecommunications.

a. Hybrid system
b. Predispositioning Theory
c. Percolation
d. Linear system

13. In mathematics and in the sciences, a _____ (plural: _____e, formulæ or _____s) is a concise way of expressing information symbolically (as in a mathematical or chemical _____), or a general relationship between quantities. One of many famous _____e is Albert Einstein's $E = mc^2$ (see special relativity

In mathematics, a _____ is a key to solve an equation with variables. For example, the problem of determining the volume of a sphere is one that requires a significant amount of integral calculus to solve.

a. 120-cell
b. 2-3 heap
c. 1-center problem
d. Formula

14. In mathematics, an _____ is a statement about the relative size or order of two objects, or about whether they are the same or not

- The notation a < b means that a is less than b.
- The notation a > b means that a is greater than b.
- The notation a ≠ b means that a is not equal to b, but does not say that one is bigger than the other or even that they can be compared in size.

In all these cases, a is not equal to b, hence, '_____'.

These relations are known as strict _____

- The notation a ≤ b means that a is less than or equal to b;
- The notation a ≥ b means that a is greater than or equal to b;

An additional use of the notation is to show that one quantity is much greater than another, normally by several orders of magnitude.

- The notation a << b means that a is much less than b.
- The notation a >> b means that a is much greater than b.

If the sense of the _____ is the same for all values of the variables for which its members are defined, then the _____ is called an 'absolute' or 'unconditional' _____. If the sense of an _____ holds only for certain values of the variables involved, but is reversed or destroyed for other values of the variables, it is called a conditional _____.

An _____ may appear unsolvable because it only states whether a number is larger or smaller than another number; but it is possible to apply the same operations for equalities to inequalities. For example, to find x for the _____ 10x > 23 one would divide 23 by 10.

a. A posteriori
b. Inequality
c. A Mathematical Theory of Communication
d. A chemical equation

15. In mathematics a _____ is an inequality which involves a linear function.

When operating in terms of real numbers, linear inequalities are the ones written in the forms

$$f(x) < b \text{ or } f(x) \leq b,$$

where f(x) is a linear functional in real numbers and b is a constant real number. Alternatively, these may be viewed as

$$g(x) < 0 \text{ or } g(x) \leq 0,$$

where g(x) is an affine function.

Chapter 7. Systems of Equations and Inequalities

a. Split-complex number
b. Generalized singular value decomposition
c. Linear inequality
d. Levi-Civita symbol

16. The term surplus is used in economics for several related quantities. The _____ is the amount that consumers benefit by being able to purchase a product for a price that is less than they would be willing to pay. The producer surplus is the amount that producers benefit by selling at a market price mechanism that is higher than they would be willing to sell for.
a. Producer surplus
b. Marginal rate of technical substitution
c. Returns to scale
d. Consumer surplus

17. The term surplus is used in economics for several related quantities. The consumer surplus is the amount that consumers benefit by being able to purchase a product for a price that is less than they would be willing to pay. The _____ is the amount that producers benefit by selling at a market price mechanism that is higher than they would be willing to sell for.
a. Producer surplus
b. Consumer surplus
c. Returns to scale
d. Marginal rate of technical substitution

18. In mathematics, a _____ is a condition that a solution to an optimization problem must satisfy. There are two types of _____s: equality _____s and inequality _____s. The set of solutions that satisfy all _____s is called the feasible set.
a. Foci
b. Concurrent
c. Decidable
d. Constraint

19. The mathematical concept of a _____ expresses the intuitive idea of deterministic dependence between two quantities, one of which is viewed as primary and the other as secondary. A _____ then is a way to associate a unique output for each input of a specified type, for example, a real number or an element of a given set.

a. Grill
b. Coherent
c. Function
d. Going up

20. In mathematics, _____ is a technique for optimization of a linear objective function, subject to linear equality and linear inequality constraints. Informally, _____ determines the way to achieve the best outcome in a given mathematical model given some list of requirements represented as linear equations.

More formally, given a polytope, and a real-valued affine function

$$f(x_1, x_2, \ldots, x_n) = c_1 x_1 + c_2 x_2 + \cdots + c_n x_n + d$$

defined on this polytope, a _____ method will find a point in the polytope where this function has the smallest value.

a. Descent direction
b. Linear programming relaxation
c. Lin-Kernighan
d. Linear programming

21. An _____ is a tree data structure in which each internal node has up to eight children. _____s are most often used to partition a three dimensional space by recursively subdividing it into eight octants. _____s are the three-dimensional analog of quadtrees.

a. Adaptive k-d tree
b. External node
c. Interval tree
d. Octree

22. In mathematics and computer science, an optimization problem is the problem of finding the best solution from all feasible solutions. More formally, an optimization problem A is a quadruple , where

- I is a set of instances;
- given an instance ⬚>, f is the set of feasible solutions;
- given an instance x and a feasible solution y of x, m denotes the measure of y, which is usually a positive real.
- g is the goal function, and is either min or max.

The goal is then to find for some instance x an _____, that is, a feasible solution y with

$$\boxed{x} >$$

For each optimization problem, there is a corresponding decision problem that asks whether there is a feasible solution for some particular measure m_0. For example, if there is a graph G which contains vertices u and v, an optimization problem might be 'find a path from u to v that uses the fewest edges'. This problem might have an answer of, say, 4.

   a. Optimal solution
   b. Approximation algorithms
   c. Exponential time
   d. Interactive proof system

23. _____ methods are common techniques to compute the equilibrium configuration of molecules. The basic idea is that a stable state of a molecular system should correspond to a local minimum of their potential energy. This kind of calculation generally starts from an arbitrary state of molecules, then the mathematical procedure of optimization allows us to move atoms in a way to reduce the net forces to nearly zero.
   a. A Mathematical Theory of Communication
   b. Energy minimization
   c. A posteriori
   d. A chemical equation

24. In mathematics, a _____ is a convincing demonstration that some mathematical statement is necessarily true. _____s are obtained from deductive reasoning, rather than from inductive or empirical arguments. That is, a _____ must demonstrate that a statement is true in all cases, without a single exception.
   a. Proof
   b. Conchoid
   c. Congruent
   d. Germ

25. _____ reductio ad impossibile is a type of logical argument where one assumes a claim for the sake of argument and derives an absurd or ridiculous outcome, and then concludes that the original claim must have been wrong as it led to an absurd result.

It makes use of the law of non-contradiction -- a statement cannot be both true and false. In some cases it may also make use of the law of excluded middle -- a statement must be either true or false.

Chapter 7. Systems of Equations and Inequalities

a. 120-cell
b. 1-center problem
c. 2-3 heap
d. Reductio ad absurdum

26. In linear algebra, a column vector or _____ is an m × 1 matrix, i.e. a matrix consisting of a single column of m elements.

$$\mathbf{x} = \begin{bmatrix} x_1 \\ x_2 \\ \vdots \\ x_m \end{bmatrix}$$

The transpose of a column vector is a row vector and vice versa.

The set of all column vectors forms a vector space which is the dual space to the set of all row vectors.

a. Split-complex number
b. Column matrix
c. Cayley-Hamilton theorem
d. Spread of a matrix

27. In mathematics, and in particular in abstract algebra, distributivity is a property of binary operations that generalises the _____ law from elementary algebra.
a. General linear group
b. Permutation
c. Distributive
d. Closure with a twist

28. In mathematics, a _____ is a rectangular table of elements, which may be numbers or, more generally, any abstract quantities that can be added and multiplied. Matrices are used to describe linear equations, keep track of the coefficients of linear transformations and to record data that depend on multiple parameters. Matrices are described by the field of _____ theory.

a. Matrix
b. Compression
c. Double counting
d. Coherent

29. In mathematics, an _____ in the sense of ring theory is a subring $\mathcal{O}$ of a ring R that satisfies the conditions

   1. R is a ring which is a finite-dimensional algebra over the rational number field $\mathbb{Q}$
   2. $\mathcal{O}$ spans R over $\mathbb{Q}$, so that $\mathbb{Q}\mathcal{O} = R$, and
   3. $\mathcal{O}$ is a lattice in R.

The third condition can be stated more accurately, in terms of the extension of scalars of R to the real numbers, embedding R in a real vector space. In less formal terms, additively $\mathcal{O}$ should be a free abelian group generated by a basis for R over $\mathbb{Q}$.

The leading example is the case where R is a number field K and $\mathcal{O}$ is its ring of integers. In algebraic number theory there are examples for any K other than the rational field of proper subrings of the ring of integers that are also _____ s.

a. Algebraic
b. Annihilator
c. Efficiency
d. Order

30. In linear algebra, a row vector or _____ is a 1 × n matrix, that is, a matrix consisting of a single row:

$$\mathbf{x} = \begin{bmatrix} x_1 & x_2 & \cdots & x_m \end{bmatrix}.$$

The transpose of a row vector is a column vector:

$$\begin{bmatrix} x_1 \\ x_2 \\ \vdots \\ x_m \end{bmatrix} = \begin{bmatrix} x_1 & x_2 & \cdots & x_m \end{bmatrix}^T.$$

The set of all row vectors forms a vector space which is the dual space to the set of all column vectors.

Row vectors are sometimes written using the following non-standard notation:

$$\mathbf{x} = \begin{bmatrix} x_1, x_2, \ldots, x_m \end{bmatrix}.$$

- Matrix multiplication involves the action of multiplying each row vector of one matrix by each column vector of another matrix.

- The dot product of two vectors a and b is equivalent to multiplying the row vector representation of a by the column vector representation of b:

$$\mathbf{a} \cdot \mathbf{b} = \begin{bmatrix} a_1 & a_2 & a_3 \end{bmatrix} \begin{bmatrix} b_1 \\ b_2 \\ b_3 \end{bmatrix}.$$

a. Woodbury matrix identity
b. Row matrix
c. Gram-Schmidt process
d. Dual vector space

31. In linear algebra, the _____ of a matrix is obtained by changing a matrix in some way.

Given the matrices A and B, where:

$$A = \begin{bmatrix} 1 & 3 & 2 \\ 2 & 0 & 1 \\ 5 & 2 & 2 \end{bmatrix}, \quad B = \begin{bmatrix} 4 \\ 3 \\ 1 \end{bmatrix}$$

Then, the _____ is written as:

$$(A|B) = \begin{bmatrix} 1 & 3 & 2 & 4 \\ 2 & 0 & 1 & 3 \\ 5 & 2 & 2 & 1 \end{bmatrix}$$

This is useful when solving systems of linear equations or the _____ may also be used to find the inverse of a matrix by combining it with the identity matrix.

Chapter 7. Systems of Equations and Inequalities

Let C be a square 2×2 matrix where $C = \begin{bmatrix} 1 & 3 \\ -5 & 0 \end{bmatrix}$

To find the inverse of C we create _____ where I is the 2×2 identity matrix.

a. Eigendecomposition
b. Unimodular polynomial matrix
c. Augmented matrix
d. Alternating sign matrix

32. In mathematics, a _____ is a constant multiplicative factor of a certain object. For example, in the expression $9x^2$, the _____ of x^2 is 9.

The object can be such things as a variable, a vector, a function, etc.

a. Stability radius
b. Coefficient
c. Fibonacci polynomials
d. Multivariate division algorithm

33. In mathematics, a _____ (or matrix element) is a function on a group of a special form, which depends on a linear representation of the group and additional data. For the case of a finite group, _____s express the action of the elements of the group in the specified representation via the entries of the corresponding matrices.

_____s of representations of Lie groups turned out to be intimately related with the theory of special functions, providing a unifying approach to large parts of this theory.

a. K-finite
b. Springer representations
c. Matrix coefficient
d. Regular representation

34. In elementary algebra, a _____ is a polynomial with two terms: the sum of two monomials. It is the simplest kind of polynomial except for a monomial.

84   Chapter 7. Systems of Equations and Inequalities

The _____ $a^2 - b^2$ can be factored as the product of two other _____s:

$a^2 - b^2$.

The product of a pair of linear _____s $ax + b$ and $cx + d$ is:

2 +x + bd.

A _____ raised to the nth power, represented as

n

can be expanded by means of the _____ theorem or, equivalently, using Pascal's triangle.

a. Rational root theorem
b. Binomial
c. Real structure
d. Cylindrical algebraic decomposition

35. In computational complexity theory, the complexity class _____ is the union of the classes in the exponential hierarchy.

$$\text{ELEMENTARY} = \text{EXP} \cup \text{2EXP} \cup \text{3EXP} \cup \cdots$$
$$= \text{DTIME}(2^n) \cup \text{DTIME}(2^{2^n}) \cup \text{DTIME}(2^{2^{2^n}}) \cup \cdots$$

The name was coined by Laszlo Kalmar, in the context of recursive functions and undecidability; most problems in it are far from _____. Some natural recursive problems lie outside _____, and are thus NONELEMENTARY.

a. A chemical equation
b. A Mathematical Theory of Communication
c. A posteriori
d. Elementary

36. In mathematics, _____ is one of the basic operations defining a vector space in linear algebra. Note that _____ is different from scalar product which is an inner product between two vectors.

More specifically, if K is a field and V is a vector space over K, then _____ is a function from K × V to V.

a. Non-negative matrix factorization
b. Jordan normal form
c. Scalar multiplication
d. Frobenius normal form

37. _____ is the mathematical operation of scaling one number by another. It is one of the four basic operations in elementary arithmetic.

_____ is defined for whole numbers in terms of repeated addition; for example, 4 multiplied by 3 can be calculated by adding 3 copies of 4 together:

$$4 + 4 + 4 = 12.$$

_____ of rational numbers and real numbers is defined by systematic generalization of this basic idea.

a. Highest common factor
b. Least common multiple
c. The number 0 is even.
d. Multiplication

38. In mathematics, _____ is a property that a binary operation can have. It means that, within an expression containing two or more of the same associative operators in a row, the order that the operations are performed does not matter as long as the sequence of the operands is not changed. That is, rearranging the parentheses in such an expression will not change its value.
a. Algebraically closed
b. Idempotence
c. Unital
d. Associativity

39. The _____ is a rule which states that when you add or multiply numbers, changing the order doesn't change the result.
a. Conditional event algebra
b. Semigroupoid
c. Coimage
d. Commutative law

40. In mathematics, the _____s are an extension of the real numbers obtained by adjoining an imaginary unit, denoted i, which satisfies:

Chapter 7. Systems of Equations and Inequalities

$$i^2 = -1.$$

Every _____ can be written in the form a + bi, where a and b are real numbers called the real part and the imaginary part of the _____, respectively.

_____s are a field, and thus have addition, subtraction, multiplication, and division operations. These operations extend the corresponding operations on real numbers, although with a number of additional elegant and useful properties, e.g., negative real numbers can be obtained by squaring _____s.

a. 1-center problem
b. 120-cell
c. Real part
d. Complex number

41. In mathematics, the term _____ has several different important meanings:

- An _____ is an equality that remains true regardless of the values of any variables that appear within it, to distinguish it from an equality which is true under more particular conditions. For this, the 'triple bar' symbol ≡ is sometimes used.
- In algebra, an _____ or _____ element of a set S with a binary operation Â· is an element e that, when combined with any element x of S, produces that same x. That is, eÂ·x = xÂ·e = x for all x in S.
  - The _____ function from a set S to itself, often denoted id or id$_S$, s the function such that i = x for all x in S. This function serves as the _____ element in the set of all functions from S to itself with respect to function composition.
  - In linear algebra, the _____ matrix of size n is the n-by-n square matrix with ones on the main diagonal and zeros elsewhere. This matrix serves as the _____ with respect to matrix multiplication.

A common example of the first meaning is the trigonometric _____

$$\sin^2 \theta + \cos^2 \theta = 1$$

which is true for all real values of θ, as opposed to

$$\cos \theta = 1,$$

which is true only for some values of θ, not all. For example, the latter equation is true when $\theta = 0$, false when $\theta = 2$

The concepts of 'additive _____' and 'multiplicative _____' are central to the Peano axioms. The number 0 is the 'additive _____' for integers, real numbers, and complex numbers. For the real numbers, for all $a \in \mathbb{R}$,

$$0 + a = a,$$

$$a + 0 = a, \text{ and}$$

$$0 + 0 = 0.$$

Similarly, The number 1 is the 'multiplicative _____' for integers, real numbers, and complex numbers.

a. Intersection
b. Identity
c. ARIA
d. Action

42. _____ is a branch of mathematics which focuses on the study of matrices. Initially a sub-branch of linear algebra, it has grown to cover subjects related to graph theory, algebra, combinatorics, and statistics as well.

The term matrix was first coined in 1848 by J.J. Sylvester as a name of an array of numbers.

a. Semi-simple operators
b. Pairing
c. Segre classification
d. Matrix theory

43. In mathematics, _____ is the operation of adding two matrices by adding the corresponding entries together. However, there is another operation which could also be considered as a kind of addition for matrices.

The usual _____ is defined for two matrices of the same dimensions.

a. Spectral theory
b. Standard basis
c. Jordan normal form
d. Matrix addition

Chapter 7. Systems of Equations and Inequalities

44. In mathematics the _____ of a set which is equipped with the operation of addition is an element which, when added to any element x in the set, yields x. One of the most familiar additive identities is the number 0 from elementary mathematics, but additive identities occur in other mathematical structures where addition is defined, such as in groups and rings.

- The _____ familiar from elementary mathematics is zero, denoted 0. For example,

    5 + 0 = 5 = 0 + 5.

- In the natural numbers N and all of its supersets, the _____ is 0. Thus for any one of these numbers n,

    n + 0 = n = 0 + n.

Let N be a set which is closed under the operation of addition, denoted +. An _____ for N is any element e such that for any element n in N,

   e + n = n = n + e.

   a. Unique factorization domain
   b. Algebraically independent
   c. Unit ring
   d. Additive identity

45. In linear algebra, the _____ or unit matrix of size n is the n-by-n square matrix with ones on the main diagonal and zeros elsewhere. It is denoted by I_n, or simply by I if the size is immaterial or can be trivially determined by the context. (In some fields, such as quantum mechanics, the _____ is denoted by a boldface one, 1; otherwise it is identical to I.)
   a. Arity
   b. Associativity
   c. Unital
   d. Identity Matrix

46. In mathematics, _____ is the operation of multiplying a matrix with either a scalar or another matrix

This is the most often used and most important way to multiply matrices.

   a. Jordan matrix
   b. Matrix calculus
   c. Logarithmic norm
   d. Matrix multiplication

47. In mathematics, the _____ of a number n is the number that, when added to n, yields zero. The _____ of n is denoted −n. For example, 7 is −7, because 7 + (−7) = 0, and the _____ of −0.3 is 0.3, because −0.3 + 0.3 = 0.
   a. Additive inverse
   b. Algebraic structure
   c. Associativity
   d. Arity

Chapter 1

1. d	2. c	3. d	4. d	5. d	6. c	7. c	8. b	9. d	10. d
11. b	12. d	13. b	14. b	15. a	16. b	17. d	18. d	19. c	20. b
21. d	22. c	23. b	24. d	25. c	26. b	27. d	28. a	29. b	30. c
31. b	32. d	33. b	34. d	35. c	36. d	37. d	38. c	39. b	40. d
41. c	42. d	43. c	44. a	45. d	46. d	47. c	48. d	49. a	50. d
51. d	52. d	53. d	54. c	55. d	56. d	57. d	58. c	59. d	60. a
61. d	62. a	63. d	64. d	65. b	66. d	67. d	68. d		

Chapter 2

1. a	2. b	3. b	4. a	5. d	6. d	7. d	8. d	9. c	10. c
11. d	12. c	13. d	14. d	15. a	16. d	17. a	18. d	19. d	20. a
21. d	22. b	23. b	24. d	25. d	26. a	27. d	28. d	29. b	30. d
31. d	32. d	33. c	34. b	35. c	36. d	37. b	38. d	39. a	40. d
41. b	42. b	43. b	44. a	45. d	46. d	47. d			

Chapter 3

1. d	2. a	3. d	4. a	5. d	6. a	7. d	8. a	9. c	10. d
11. d	12. b	13. b	14. c	15. b	16. d	17. c	18. a		

Chapter 4

1. d	2. b	3. d	4. d	5. d	6. d	7. d	8. d	9. d	10. a
11. d	12. c	13. d	14. d	15. d	16. a	17. b	18. d	19. d	20. d
21. a	22. a	23. a	24. d	25. a	26. b	27. d	28. a	29. a	30. d
31. d	32. d	33. d	34. b	35. d	36. b	37. d	38. d	39. d	40. a
41. d	42. d	43. d	44. d	45. d	46. d	47. b	48. d		

Chapter 5

1. d	2. c	3. a	4. a	5. b	6. d	7. a	8. c	9. d	10. a
11. a	12. d	13. c	14. a						

Chapter 6

1. d	2. b	3. a	4. b	5. a	6. d	7. d	8. d	9. b	10. d
11. d	12. d	13. b	14. d	15. d	16. d	17. a	18. b	19. c	20. d
21. b	22. a	23. a	24. d	25. b	26. d	27. d	28. d	29. c	30. c
31. d	32. a	33. c	34. d	35. d	36. b				

Chapter 7

1. d	2. d	3. a	4. c	5. d	6. a	7. b	8. d	9. c	10. d
11. a	12. d	13. d	14. b	15. c	16. d	17. a	18. d	19. c	20. d
21. d	22. a	23. b	24. a	25. d	26. b	27. c	28. a	29. d	30. b
31. c	32. b	33. c	34. b	35. d	36. c	37. d	38. d	39. d	40. d
41. b	42. d	43. d	44. d	45. d	46. d	47. a			

www.ingramcontent.com/pod-product-compliance
Lightning Source LLC
Chambersburg PA
CBHW081847230426

43669CB00018B/2857